The Instructional Leader's Guide to Strategic Conversations with Teachers

How to provide customized feedback to teachers that actually helps them get better at teaching

ROBYN R. JACKSON, PH.D

www.mindstepsinc.com
Washington, DC

Published by Mindsteps™ Inc.

ISBN: 978-0-9789772-4-5

Acknowledgements

I owe much of what I have learned about effective instructional leadership over the years to some very smart people:

- Michael Zarchin for never letting me forget the importance of moving methodically and honoring relationships, Frank Stetson who taught me the importance of balance and of building trust, Steve Bedford who showed me how to use data to help others make better instructional decisions, and Linda Ferrell who showed me how to run a meeting where work actually gets done.
- The visionary administrators with whom I have had the honor of working over the last few years -- Valda Valbrun, Nicole Brown, Dr. Donna Redmond Jones, Traci Townsend, Khadija Barkley, Dr. Genevieve Floyd, Silvia Morrison, Lawrence Pendergast, Gene Pinkard, and Rasheed Meadows. I learn so much by watching the work they do.
- Linda Natale, who pointed me to countless resources and whose insightful comments on this book helped clarify my thinking and sharpen my focus. Max Thompson, whose work I have admired for a long time and who selflessly mentors me. Claire Lambert, whose masterful ability to hold reflective conversations helped me think through and refine many of the ideas in this book. She is a marvelous editor and friend. Donna Graves who is one of the most well-read people I know. Our conversations continue to expand my thinking. Cynthia Gill whose strategic conversations with me keep me focused. Kenyatta Dorey Graves, who provided such valuable feedback on many of the workbooks in this series.

He continues to challenge and broaden my understanding and really should write a book himself.

- And finally, the mindsteps leadership team: John, Saundra, Melissa, Doug, Shawn, and most of all Sheri whose masterful management of mindsteps' day-to-day operations makes it possible for me to keep writing.

Table of Contents

Preface

Four Leadership Scenarios

MRS. HENDERSON

Mitchell walked out of Mrs. Henderson's fifth-grade classroom and headed back to his office. He had just completed a formal observation of her class and Mitchell was worried by what he saw. Mrs. Henderson spent the first 16 minutes of class taking attendance and collecting homework. Once she began her instruction, the students talked through the warm up, which had little to do with the posted objective. Most of the students were off task during the lesson activity and instead of helping them get back on task, Mrs. Henderson plowed through the lesson, occasionally warning students that she would give them lunch detention if they didn't get their act together.

But as much as he knew he needed to give Mrs. Henderson feedback, he dreaded the post-observation conference. Mrs. Henderson was a veteran teacher who believed she was effective in the classroom. Her problem, she always complained, was that the students were lazy. Over the 18 years she had been teaching, she had received positive evaluations from her former principals. She was active in the teacher's union and had recently earned her EdD from a local university. Mitchell knew if he gave her the feedback she needed, she would immediately call the union and trash him in the teachers' lounge. It was a headache he didn't want to have.

MR. LOCKE

Cassandra sat in her office stunned by what she had just heard. A parent had called and reported that Mr. Locke, the AP chemistry teacher, had not conducted one lab the entire year -- and it was February. The students would be facing the AP exam in just 3 short months and without doing any labs, they were desperately behind. Mr. Locke was a fairly new teacher and this was his first year teaching AP chemistry. He was enthusiastic and well-liked by the students and his colleagues. He worked hard at learning the curriculum and eagerly attended the professional development opportunities provided by the district. Earlier that year, he had struggled with classroom management but was now working hard to get his students focused on learning. Cassandra looked at the stack of papers waiting to be graded on her desk. She had her own classes to teach and her own students to manage. She didn't have time to teach Mr. Locke's classes too. She knew it was going to take a considerable amount of time to help Mr. Locke and his students catch up and she had no idea where she would find the time to work with Mr. Locke and get him back on track. "Why did I ever let them convince me to be department chair," she sighed as she reached for the AP Chemistry Course Guide.

MS. PAULSON

Marla walked around the room and collected the left-over handouts. She had just finished presenting at the faculty meeting and she was livid. Weeks earlier, her principal had shared with her the dismal reading scores their students had earned on the last state test. She asked Marla, who was the reading specialist, if she would share a few reading strategies with the staff at the next faculty meeting. Marla had spent hours researching best practices, created handouts with strategies teachers could immediately use with their students, and put together a PowerPoint presentation with the school's data and a plan of action. The last part of the meeting was devoted to teachers working in small groups to develop a plan for how they would raise their students' reading scores this school year. All of the teachers were enthusiastic about the information and immediately got to work. All of the teachers except Ms. Paulson. Ms. Paulson read a magazine throughout most of the presentation and when the teachers began working in groups, she reluctantly joined a group near where she was sitting but contributed little to the discussion. It had been that way all year. Ms. Paulson would do what was required, but nothing more and yet, her students' scores were well below the rest of the school. "She's so irritating!" Marla fumed as she put the AV cart into the closet. "What's it going to take to get her on board with the rest of us?"

MR. TERRELL

Scott scanned the latest test results and smiled. The scores were up overall but one teacher's scores really stood out. Mr. Terrell's students had outperformed the other students in their grade by 10 percentage points. "I'm not surprised," Scott chuckled. Mr. Terrell was one of those rare teachers you'd die to have in your building. Not only was he an excellent instructor, but he cheerfully took on any task he was assigned. He was a joy to have on the staff and made a tremendous difference in the lives of the students. Parents clamored to have their students in his class. Mr. Terrell also sponsored the chess club after school and came in on the weekend to tutor students who needed extra help. Lately however, Mr. Terrell seemed a little bored. He still did whatever was asked of him but Scott sensed he needed a new challenge and worried that Mr. Terrell would look for that challenge at another school. Scott reached for a $10.00 gift-card to Starbucks and sheet of his personal stationary. "Great job on those test scores," he scribbled quickly. "Keep up the good work!" As he put the note and the gift card into the envelope, Scott felt a little uneasy. It seemed such a small reward for all the work Mr. Terrell had done. He wished he could find a way to really show Mr. Terrell how much he valued him.

Chances are, if you are an instructional leader you have similar challenges. Whether you are a principal, assistant principal, staff development teacher, instructional coach, specialist, or district-level leader, you have at one time or another struggled with how to share feedback with the teachers you serve. We may be experts on helping students improve, but helping the adults in our buildings improve can present a real challenge.

Instructional leadership, like teaching itself, is a difficult, complex process. And, if you are anything like most instructional leaders, you have had little in the way of training. How do you provide teachers with effective feedback? How do you structure conversations with the teachers in your building that will make a real difference in their teaching performance?

The good news is that there is a way to help each of the teachers in the opening vignettes and every teacher you serve improve. This book will show you how to do just that. You will learn how to:

- move away from ineffective supervisory models to one designed to help you quickly assess and understand the primary needs of your instructional staff.
- strategically apply your leadership skills to motivate and support teachers to improve their instruction
- help teachers make the connection between their effective effort and tangible improvements in student learning.

At the heart of this model is the idea of strategic conversations.

What is a Strategic Conversation?

Strategic conversations are a series of targeted, individualized interactions with teachers designed to help them significantly improve the impact of their teaching behaviors on student achievement. Unlike typical supervisory feedback, strategic conversations move in two directions. Both you and the teacher actively participate in identifying the problem and determining the solution to instructional challenges. And, strategic conversations provide teachers the support and structure that allow them eventually to make their own choices about how they will resolve their instructional challenges and grow as professionals.

Strategic conversations rely on four conversational approaches-- Reflecting, Facilitating, Coaching, and Directing. Each of these approaches will garner a different outcome depending on who the teacher is, and what the teacher needs. No one conversation will be a magic bullet. It is the effective combination of these four conversational approaches, matched to the teacher and the situation that will help you move teachers towards specific instructional goals.

What makes strategic conversations so effective is that rather than prescribing one approach to help a specific type of teacher, strategic conversations provide you with several options for working with each teacher based on the teacher's need, situation, and the outcome you are working towards. Strategic conversations don't just depend on a single interaction. Instead, strategic conversations help you structure a series of interactions with teachers that help them make incremental, consistent growth towards becoming more effective in the classroom.

These conversations are by no means easy. If the teachers in your building have been receiving unclear feedback for years, it may be difficult at first for them to receive more frequent and targeted feedback. They may initially resist your efforts. But, by using strategic conversations, you can develop relationships with teachers where they see you as a partner rather than a judge. In this way, you will be best positioned to help teachers develop the will and the skill to constantly improve their practice.

The key to managing these conversations is to carefully plan your approach ahead of time. This book will help you think through your overall goals, and the individual needs of each teacher, and then strategically select the best conversational approach to help you meet both. Without planning, you may abandon an approach midway through or shift to a conversational approach that is inappropriate for the teacher. Without prior planning, you may find at the end of the conversation not only have you strayed from your goals, but you have also damaged the relationship with the teacher in the process.

Conducting strategic conversations is not a skill in and of itself; rather it is a repertoire of skills effectively matched to the individual needs of the teachers you serve. Although this book provides a step-by-step guide to structuring these conversations, they are by no means as easy or neat as they may appear on paper. Facilitating teacher development can be a messy process. Just as with any serious conversation that shapes an important relationship, things can get complicated. This book won't eliminate the mess, but it will help you manage it.

Ultimately, this book will help you develop a long-term plan for how you will work with each teacher you serve. You will learn how to collect data to effectively diagnose where teachers are and then match your leadership approach to each individual teacher's needs. You will learn how to structure individual conversations as well as design a series of interactions with each teacher so you can consistently and effectively help them improve their practice. And, you will learn how to manage it all by prioritizing your goals to determine which teachers to work with first.

How to Use this Book

As you read this book, you are going to develop a system to have the right kind of conversations with each teacher you encounter to get the outcome you want. Just like you use many pathways to help your students to improve their performance, there are several different pathways to getting teachers to improve theirs. Thus, not only will you learn how to apply each of the four conversational approaches, you will learn how to quickly figure out what kind of teacher you are facing, determine the best conversational approach to help the teacher improve, and how to follow up with other conversations to keep the teacher moving in the right direction.

While some of you might want to jump right into learning how to conduct strategic conversations, there is some internal work you will need to do first. If you want to engage in these conversations successfully, the first step is to uncover any outdated and ineffective paradigms you may have about what effective instructional leadership should look like. Chapter One explains the difference between strategic conversations and traditional supervisory feedback and discusses the foundational dispositions you must have if your strategic conversations are going to be effective. You will need to think through these foundations and consider your own beliefs and experiences before you start apply strategic conversations with your staff members.

Chapter Two shows you how to diagnose the individual needs of the teachers you serve. It provides you with a breakdown of the four types of teachers, and gives you strategies for how to recognize them and meet them where they are. The chapter ends by explaining the various data collection methods you can use to gather the information you will need to select the best conversational approach for each teacher.

Chapter Three describes the strategic conversations – reflecting, facilitating, coaching, and directing. You will learn the purpose of each conversation, when the conversation is appropriate, and how to apply it. You will also discover how to tailor each conversation to the needs of the four types of teachers. Chapter Three contains various worksheets and guidelines to help you plan your conversations ahead of time.

Chapter Four shows you how to develop a plan to apply what you have learned. You will learn how to combine the four types of conversations to design a series of interactions over time tailored to each teacher with whom you are working. And, you find suggestions for how to sequence conversations in order to have the biggest impact with each of the four types of teachers. You will also learn how to decide which teachers to work with first, how to manage it all, and how to track your progress.

Throughout the book we will revisit the teachers we met at the beginning of this chapter. At the end of each chapter, you will practice applying what you are learning about strategic conversations with Mrs. Henderson, Mr. Locke, Ms. Paulson, and Mr. Terrell.

The Conclusion has tips for staying focused throughout the process. You can use these as reminders of why strategic conversations are important and as encouragement to help you stay the course. The appendices contain more detailed explanations of some of the data collections strategies mentioned in the book. You can learn to conduct informal and formal observations and more effective walk-throughs using the step-by-step guides and templates.

We have also created a companion website where you can download other resources to support you as apply strategic conversations at your school. Visit www.mindstepsinc.com/conversations.asp to download resources available exclusively to readers of this book.

As always, we want to hear from you. After you've tried the strategies in this book, do drop us a line at **info@mindstepsinc.com** to let us know how you used the book, what parts you found most helpful, and what parts you found most difficult. We also want to hear your success stories so tell us how you used the strategies in this book and how they made a difference in your teaching and in the lives of your students. And, if you would like a Mindsteps™ Coach to come to your school district and work with your staff on these strategies, give us a call at **1-888-565-8881** or send us an email. We would love to help.

Step One

GETTING READY FOR STRATEGIC CONVERSATIONS

Strategic Conversations versus Traditional Supervisory Feedback

SUPERVISORY FEEDBACK...	STRATEGIC CONVERSATIONS...
Uses a static metric to determine teacher needs i.e. new versus veteran teachers or math versus English teachers.	Use a dynamic metric such as the will/skill continuum to diagnose teacher needs.
Operates under the assumption that the leader is the expert.	Operate under the assumption of shared expertise
Applies the same approach for multiple teachers.	Use different approaches based on each teacher's needs.
Provides sporadic feedback usually tied to formal evaluations.	Provide ongoing feedback tied to professional growth and development.
is reactive.	are proactive.

We are expected to differentiate our instruction in the classroom. It is accepted as common knowledge that we have to adjust our instructional practice to meet the needs of all of the learners in the classroom. But, when it comes to instructional leadership, our approach is often the one-size-fits-all.

Most books on instructional leadership focus on how to give effective supervisory feedback designed to convey your leadership vision, establish norms, reward good teaching, and remove ineffective teachers from your building. They show you how to write vision statements, develop missions and core values, conduct observations, create improvement plans, and maintain a paper trail to get rid of underperforming teachers. Rarely do they show you how to help an underperforming teacher get better.

Some books go a little further and attempt to describe different types of teachers and how to approach each one. They prescribe a leadership approach for each teacher based on providing supervisory feedback and developing improvement plans with suggested activities to help the teacher become more effective in the classroom.

At the heart of all of these books is the idea that instructional leadership is based on creating and conveying your vision, developing a plan for realizing your vision, and providing the appropriate supervisory feedback to help teachers reach your vision.

This book will not show you how to provide more effective supervisory feedback. In fact, it is based on the belief that supervisory feedback is ineffective, inefficient, and impractical given the very diverse needs of the teachers in your building. Instead, this book will help you eliminate supervisory feedback and replace it with strategic conversations that motivate and enable teachers in your building to significantly improve their instructional practice.

Strategic conversations are much more dynamic than supervisory feedback. Instead of one tightly scripted form of feedback often found in supervisory models, strategic conversations give you four options of the kind of feedback you can give at any one time – reflective, facilitative, coaching, or directive. What makes these conversations strategic is not that you simply match one conversational type to each kind of teacher you meet. It is that you understand the effect each conversation will have on each type of teacher and then plan a combination or series of conversations over time that will have the biggest impact on helping each teacher improve.

Strategic conversations rely on the idea that every teacher can get better at teaching with the right kind of practice and support. As Roland S. Barth (2005) puts it, "If we truly believe that all children can learn, then we must believe that all educators can learn, even in the face of contrary evidence." (p. 122)

Rather than focus on getting rid of underperforming teachers, strategic conversations focus on creating a culture of constant growth and improvement where teachers are given the support they need to get better at teaching. Yes, it is important to eliminate mediocre or poor teaching, but the best way to get rid of mediocre or poor teaching is to help those teachers improve.

Supervisory conversations usually begin with a classroom observation. Under the supervisory model, the observation process becomes a chore, little more than a ritual in which we and teachers engage once a year, both of us sticking to well-rehearsed scripts. Outside of the observation process we just don't have the time or perhaps even the expertise to provide feedback on instruction that is tailored to our teachers' individual needs.

Another problem with supervisory conversations is that the type of feedback we are taught to give is often vague and provides little direction as to how teachers can improve. If a teacher is doing well, we provide non-specific praise such as "great job" or "meets standard" that does little to show teachers what they can do to maintain or even improve their successful performance. If a teacher's instructional approach is not working, we either provide prescriptions that do not invite the teacher to be a part of the solution, or we buffer our negative assessments in unclear language.

Many of us think we are being kind by writing observation reports and evaluations that sandwich the truth about poor performance between lukewarm praise. We are taught to say things like, "Although Ms. Jones is a very nice person and works hard to engage her students, not all of her students were paying attention to the lesson. Still, the lesson was well designed and had many opportunities for hands on activities." Well which one is it? Was the lesson effective or wasn't it? Based on this assessment, what is it that Ms. Jones is supposed to work on? How can Ms. Jones improve?

Year after year, teachers receive these vague assessments as their only feedback, little if any of which is useful for their professional growth. In fact, it may even convey that their performance is just fine as it is.

Strategic conversations change that. They do not rely on observation reports or evaluations as the only form of feedback; they allow instructional leaders the chance to provide ongoing feedback throughout the year.

Supervisory conversations often seem more designed to provide a single and final evaluation of a teacher's performance and cookie cutter prescriptions for improvement. Strategic conversations provide teachers with ongoing direct and honest assessments of their current performance and help them develop the skills and the disposition they need to improve and meet or exceed the standards. The feedback is not a one shot deal. It is part of a continuous conversation on effective instruction and student achievement. And, because this feedback is tailored to teachers' individual needs, it is more likely to make a real difference in their practice.

Strategic conversations emphasize problem solving among staff. The instructional leader is not the problem solver; the instructional leader facilitates problem solving among teachers. Strategic conversations give teachers the responsibility of managing their own professional growth and solving their own instructional challenges. Strategic conversations are based on the assumption that teachers are trying to do the best they can. The role of the instructional leader is to help teachers discover the root cause of their instructional challenges and to help teachers resolve these challenges themselves.

At the heart of strategic conversations is a relationship. In the same way that students work best with teachers with whom they have a positive relationship, teachers work best with leaders with whom they have a positive relationship. Strategic conversations help you establish trust and maintain it -- even when you are sharing really difficult feedback. When teachers feel safe, they are more likely to take the steps they need to improve.

Supervision in a school district often does not look like this. In fact, when you were a teacher, you may have never experienced this kind of feedback yourself. Strategic conversations represent a whole new way of approach to instructional leadership; therefore, how you think about instructional leadership and giving feedback to teachers will also have to be different. When you choose to use strategic conversations rather than traditional supervisory feedback, you are making a commitment to being a different kind of instructional leader. So, before you begin the process, here are some ideas you will need to consider and ultimately embrace.

The Foundational Beliefs of Strategic Conversations

Strategic conversations are built upon a foundation of understandings, beliefs, and commitments. Before you can effectively engage in strategic conversations, you will need to take some time to consider these foundations and ultimately make several commitments yourself. Only then are you ready to use the strategic conversational approach with teachers.

The first foundation of strategic conversations is an understanding of what makes good instruction. This understanding will not only help you recognize effective instruction when you see it; it will also help you recognize when effective instruction is not taking place and identify areas for improvement. Taking time to fully articulate what effective instruction looks like will give your work a sense of purpose, direction, and coherence. For a comprehensive picture of what effective instruction looks like, read *Never Work Harder than Your Students and Other Principles of Great Teaching*[1].

Along with this grasp of what makes effective instruction, you need to actually believe that teachers can, with effective instructional leadership and support, improve their practice. If you have only experienced supervisory feedback and rarely witnessed improvement, it may be hard to believe any teacher can improve. But, simply by choosing to use strategic conversations, you have already begun to shift your beliefs. The more you persist with strategic conversations, the more you will begin to believe that any teacher can change because you will see teachers improve. For more help on adjusting your beliefs and expectations, read pages 77-101 in *Never Work Harder than Your Students and Other Principles of Great Teaching.*

Next, you need to establish a shared understanding of what constitutes good instruction by clarifying what you mean when you use certain terms. For instance, many supervisory conversations are centered on "meeting standard." This term is used both

1. Jackson, R. (2009). *Never Work Harder than Your Students and Other Principles of Great Teaching.* Alexandria, VA: ASCD.

to address what the students must do and what the teacher must do. Although the standards are published and in the hands of every teacher, the term "standard" itself is often a fuzzy notion. Do we mean all of the standards? Do we mean the minimum standard requirement? Do we mean a specific standard or group of standards? In a strategic conversation, it is important that when you use a term, you are clear and you make clear to the person with whom you are speaking exactly what you mean. It is equally important that you ask the person with whom you are conversing what they mean when they use certain terms so you are both clear. An excellent reference book to help you clarify teaching terms is *The Skillful Teacher*[2].

Because strategic conversations are often uncomfortable, you and the person with whom you are conversing may naturally want to avoid them. Therefore, another foundation for effective strategic conversations is the commitment to remain engaged even when the conversation reaches a difficult phase, and even when the other person has not made the same commitment. Strategic conversations are ongoing. Not every phase of the conversation will result in closure. Therefore, you have to commit to remain engaged in the conversation, to follow up, to return to the teacher after a difficult point and resume the conversation. Otherwise little real progress will be made.

One way to help you remain engaged is to develop a plan for what conversations you will have and how you will have them. Chapter Four contains a worksheet and step-by-step instructions for how to chart a series of strategic conversations matched to the individual needs of the teacher. By creating a long-term plan of action, you are more likely to remain engaged because you have anticipated the difficult times and have planned for how you will work through and beyond them.

A fourth foundation of strategic conversations is truth. Although it seems obvious that you will need to be truthful, honesty in many situations may be more difficult than you think. It's hard to share honest feedback with your colleagues when that feedback is not positive. It's not easy to tell a teacher who has been receiving glowing feedback from former leaders that they need to make serious adjustments in their instructional practice. It is difficult to tell someone with whom you have worked side-by-side for years that they will have to improve in some area. It is really tough to provide instructional feedback to someone you consider a friend. You don't want to offend the other person, so you may try to sugar-coat your feedback. But, doing so is ultimately even more offensive. Unless you provide honest feedback to teachers, they cannot act on your feedback and improve their practice. As tough as it is to share the

2. Saphier, J. & Gower, R. (2008). *The Skillful Teacher.* Acton, MA: Research for Better Teaching, Inc.

truth sometimes, it is the only way teachers will get the information they need to improve. To help you speak the truth Chapter Two has strategies for collecting data and sharing it with teachers objectively.

Because strategic conversations are ongoing, and because they often require you to share truths that are uncomfortable, you will have to increase your tolerance for discomfort. There will not always be closure after each conversation. Sometimes teachers will not want to hear what you have to share with them. And, because the conversation goes both ways, you will not always want to hear what teachers have to say to you. To help increase your tolerance for discomfort, the worksheets in this book will help you plan your strategic conversations ahead of time and Chapter Four will help you develop a long-term plan for the progression of strategic conversations with each teacher. This planning will keep you focused on your long-term goals rather than your short-term discomfort.

Finally, if you are going to be effective at strategic conversations, you will need to withhold personal judgments and biases and focus on what is best for students. Because strategic conversations are based on the belief that every teacher can get better at teaching, you cannot give up on a teacher or hold back support because you do not like the teacher personally. Strategic conversations require you to give every teacher the best chance to improve, even when it doesn't look as if they ever will. To help you objectively decide which teachers you will work with, Chapter Four helps you develop a plan prioritized by school goals and students' needs rather than your own personal preferences.

Your growth in these foundations will happen over time as you continue to apply the strategic conversational approaches and refine your own instructional leadership skills. You may agree with many of the intellectually, but find that at times, your professional practice contradicts one or more of these beliefs. If you reach a difficult point or find yourself having trouble applying strategic conversations effectively, it is likely because you are struggling with one of these foundational beliefs. Rather than work on fixing the individual conversation, revisit these foundations first and figure out where you need to make adjustments in your own belief system. You will find that once you do, the rest will be much easier.

The Four Types of Strategic Conversations

Once you have established these foundations, you are ready to begin the process of matching the type of conversation to the type of teacher. The first step is to diagnose the needs of the teachers you serve. Once you have pinpointed the level of will and skill of each of your teachers, you can decide on a conversational approach that best matches the needs of the individual teacher. The approach you select will rely on a combination of the four types of strategic conversations: Reflecting, Facilitating, Coaching, and Directing.

Reflective conversations help teachers make *connections* between their behavior or attitudes and student achievement. Facilitative conversations help teachers make commitments to improve their instructional practice and give them the supports to do so. Coaching conversations help teaches make changes in their instructional practice so that students are more likely to succeed. You work with teachers to help them develop the skills they need and get access to the resources they require. Directive conversations require teachers to make corrections in their teaching practice. They require much more involvement from you both in identifying the problem and recommending solutions. And, you will need to follow up to hold teachers accountable for making the changes you have asked them to make.

There is a time and a place for each of these conversations. The secret to what makes them work is not in any one type of conversation; it is in how you combine the different conversations as you work with teachers over time to help them improve. Change may happen after one conversation, but it is more likely to happen after a series of ongoing conversations. The approach you use will depend on the needs you have identified during your assessment. The next chapter shows you in detail how to assess your staff. The rest of this book will help you apply these conversational approaches and match them to the individual needs of your staff.

Step Two

ASSESS THE NEEDS OF THE TEACHERS YOU SERVE

Before you can design a series of strategic conversations individualized for each teacher you serve, you need to quickly and accurately assess the needs of your staff. If you cannot tell what your staff needs, then you cannot tailor your leadership approach to meet their needs.

Assessing your staff is not nearly as complicated as you might think. You don't need to use some sophisticated analysis tool or spend months collecting data. You can assess your staff's needs very quickly by looking at two key areas: will and skill.

Will and Skill

Teaching is a combination of will and skill. It is not enough to simply understand their subject matter and the pedagogical methods of teaching, effective teachers also genuinely care about their students and work hard to improve their craft. Effective teaching is the intersection between will and skill

Will has to do with a teacher's motivation and resolve to do what is best on behalf of students. A teacher's will is an outgrowth of his/her belief system. It is directly related to what they believe about children, about teaching, about how children learn, and about school itself and it is often the result of to the kind of support – or lack of support – they get over their years of teaching.

Although you can listen to what a teacher says in order to get clues about his will, it is even more important to look at what the teacher does. Does the teacher's indicate he believes all students can learn? Does the teacher's behavior reveal a commitment to his students' mental, physical, and emotional welfare? Does the teacher seem willing to do whatever it takes to ensure that all his students are successful? Does the teacher demonstrate high expectations for all his students? Is he reflective about his practice? Does he seek out and accept feedback? Does he use feedback to improve his instructional practice?

Skill has to do with both pedagogical and content area knowledge. Does the teacher know her subject or content area? Does she demonstrate that she has an understanding of the learning needs of her students? Does she effectively manage student behavior? Does she understand the curriculum? Can she make connections between the curriculum and the assessments she uses? Does she track student progress? Are her students learning? Both content knowledge and pedagogical knowledge are important. If a teacher has high content knowledge but little pedagogical knowledge she cannot help students learn what she knows. And, if a teacher understands how to teach but does not understand his subject then he will not be able to help students learn that content. Teaching skill then is a combination of both knowing your subject and knowing how to help others learn your subject.

The teachers in your building will be at various places on the will/skill continuum. Some teachers will have a sincere desire to improve their craft but need more support in understanding their subject area. Some teachers will have a thorough understanding of their content area but have become disillusioned with teaching. Others will excel both in their pedagogical knowledge and in their commitment to their craft. And, still others will struggle both in terms of their commitment to teaching and in terms of their teaching skill. Each of these teachers has different needs and to attempt to support them in the same way not only

Assessing Your Staff

Think about your staff. Then, using the table below, plot each staff member along the skill/ will continuum. (or skip ahead to the descriptions and return to jot down names of the teachers who fit each category)

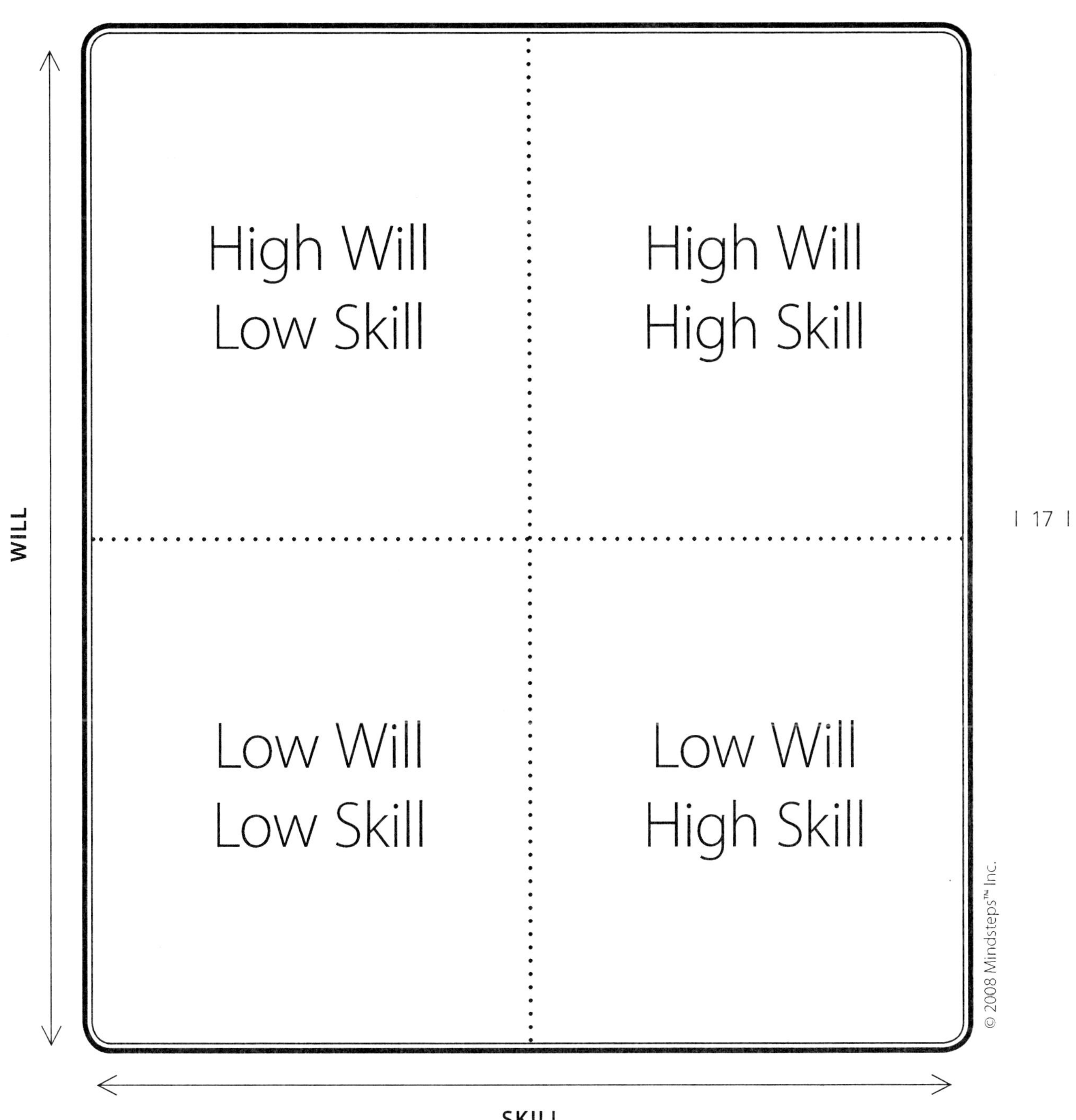

fails to address their needs, but can lead to cynicism or even resentment of your efforts at instructional leadership. Thus, in order to determine the best approach to instructional leadership for each teacher, you must first determine where your teachers are on the will/skill continuum.

The Four Types of Teachers

Each quadrant on the will/skill grid represents a different type of teacher. Each type of teacher has a different set of needs and requires a different instructional leadership approach. Keep in mind, the will/skill continuum is dynamic. Teachers may move from one quadrant to the next as they move through their careers, change courses, switch schools, move to different levels, or experience different events in their personal lives. Teachers will also move among the quadrants as a result of your working with them and helping them improve. Therefore, your assessment of where teachers are must also be dynamic and you will have to revisit your initial assessment often not only as you gather more data and develop a more complete picture of a teacher's will and skill but also as a way to track your progress once your work with teachers begins to take effect.

LOW WILL/LOW SKILL:

Low Will/Low Skill teachers not only struggle with their content area and their pedagogy, but they have little or no motivation to improve. Without either the skill or the will to deliver effective instruction in the classroom, these teachers can do students great harm. Thus, it is important for instructional leaders to act quickly to move these teachers either to another quadrant or out of the building.

Often, it is difficult to understand the kind of negative impact these teachers can have on students. We tend to tolerate Low Will/Low Skill teachers because they are so difficult to move. Unlike the Low Will/High Skill teacher who acts as a saboteur and thus can quickly earn our ire, Low Will/Low Skill teachers do not tend to buck the status quo. Theirs is a more passive resistance to change and as a result, many instructional leaders tend to tolerate them or at best, work around them, and spend their energy focusing on the more troublesome teachers.

Low Will/Low Skill teachers are often assigned remedial classes or other classes that are low profile in the building.

Low Will/Low Skill teachers SAY:

- I only have three years to retirement so I am just biding my time.
- I am too old to change.
- Just tell me what you want me to do.
- I went into teaching so I could have the summers off.
- I am happy with things just the way they are.
- I've seen these educational fads come and go so there is no use in changing the way I teach.
- My students are low, they can't be expected to do X.
- My principal/department head/team leader just doesn't like me or the way I teach.

Low Will/Low Skill teachers DO:

- Read the paper or complete Crossword Puzzles during staff meetings.
- Show up late to meetings and contribute little if anything to the discussion.
- Are the last ones in the building and the first ones to leave.
- Do not seek out professional development activities.
- Use the same lesson plans year after year.
- Spend their planning period socializing or running errands.
- Rarely participate in professional development over the summer.
- Are resistant to feedback (this resistance may be passive).
- Focus on coverage rather than mastery.
- May rationalize instructional short comings by pointing out the other extra-curricular support they provide in the school building such as coaching, sponsoring a club or activity, or ordering supplies.
- Have a hard time articulating the connections between classroom activities and the content or skills students need to master.

- Fail to anticipate elements of the lesson that will confuse students.
- Give unclear directions to students.

Strategies for Low Will/Low Skill Teachers

- Identify which will be easier to tackle first, will or skill, and start there.
- Share your passion and commitment for teaching and learning in both formal and informal conversations.
- Use multiple sources of data such as lesson plans, student artifacts, student performance on standardized tests and other measures, and both formal and informal observations to identify patterns and gaps in performance.
- Use frequent informal observations as a way of holding them accountable.
- Give them more challenging assignments, provide them with the necessary support, and then hold them accountable for the work they must do.
- Stop enabling LWLS teachers by providing them with a lightened academic load and less challenging assignments.
- Focus on the choices teachers make in the classroom and their impact on students.
- Point out missed opportunities to challenge students, provide more rigor, or otherwise engage students in the classroom.
- Ask to see lesson and unit plans regularly and look for evidence that they are being implemented in the classroom.
- Ask to see samples of student work and get the teacher to explain the connections between this product and the skill or content he is teaching.
- Ask teachers to present evidence of the way in which they keep themselves current in the field and discuss how this learning is evidenced in their instructional practice.
- Conduct a career coaching conversation focused on their aspirations, career goals, and professional achievement goals. Ask teachers to project where they see themselves in five years and how they see their current performance helping them to achieve their goals.
- Conduct frequent informal hallway conversations about teaching and learning.
- Provide directives for improvement.
- Focus some reflective conversations on non-classroom areas of performance such as collaboration with colleagues, professional learning opportunities, and professional duties and responsibilities.

LOW WILL/HIGH SKILL:

Low Will/High Skill teachers have the pedagogical and content area knowledge to be effective teachers; however, they are not motivated to improve their instructional practice and typically have fairly low expectations of their students. They are able but unwilling.

Low Will/High Skill teachers tend to be the saboteurs in your building. They have the skill set to be effective teachers but for a variety of reasons, refuse to do what is best on behalf of students. They will typically have well-planned lessons and usually have a good grasp of the content, but their relationships with their students and their colleagues are often poor. Additionally, these teachers refuse to take ownership of their students' performance and therefore resist feedback.

Many Low Will/High Skill teachers used to be High Will/High Skill teachers. But, over the years, they may have experienced some disappointment or frustration that has sapped them of their will. The bad news is many of these teachers have let their frustration turn into cynicism. The good news is that if they were once High Will/High Skill teachers, they can become High Will/High Skill teachers again.

Low Will/High Skill teachers SAY:

- That won't work.
- We've already tried that.
- It's not my fault.
- I've done everything I could.
- When are we going to hold the students responsible?
- My students just don't care.
- There isn't time.
- We always get more to do, nothing is ever taken away.
- What's the point? I get the same paycheck as the person who leaves when the bell rings. When is someone going to do something about those teachers?
- Students weren't like this 10, 20, 30 years ago.
- They should have learned this last year.
- They don't know the basics.

Low Will/High Skill teachers DO:

- Blame the parents.
- Blame the students.
- Refuse to take ownership for their problems.
- Resent reflective conversations.
- Focus on tweaking their lesson plans rather than on building relationships with students.
- Work late.
- Come the staff meetings on time but carry on sidebar conversations.
- Take leave on staff meeting and professional development days.
- Tend to have low expectations of students (or ability based beliefs – the smart kids will do great, we're wasting our time with the ones who will never get it).
- Prefer content-related professional development versus professional development that addresses pedagogical issues.

- Spend a lot of time denying or shifting blame.
- Rarely send students to the office but when they do, it is usually for seemingly minor or arbitrary infractions.
- Close their doors.
- Plan alone.
- Teach advanced classes.

May have received positive performance evaluations in the past and therefore may resist your initial efforts at helping them improve.

Strategies for Low Will/High Skill Teachers

- Focus on their strengths and arrange their work so their strengths are maximized.
- Match them to tasks that take advantage of their strengths.
- Regularly recognize and celebrate their accomplishments.
- Model giving input in a positive manner.
- Seek to find a common ground in terms of beliefs on which you can build.
- First build rapport, then ask for change.
- Try to find out the underlying reasons for the lack of will.
- Work to develop ownership rather than buy-in.
- Use data to support recommendations.
- Use informal observations as a way of building rapport and for initiating conversations about instructional practices and beliefs.
- Challenge negative statements by asking the teacher probing questions rather than by expressing outright disagreement. Use reflective conversations to help the teacher see what is wrong with the statement.
- Focus on patterns of behaviors rather than discrete incidents.
- Conduct frequent informal hallway conversations that solicit their teaching beliefs and attitudes.
- Conduct frequent, informal hallway conversations about their lives and their concerns.
- Leverage favors.
- Begin with recommendations for improvement but if these are not implemented, move to directives.
- Involve another trusted administrator or supervisor to increase credibility.
- Make goal setting a collaborative process.
- Prompt them to invite you to class when they try a new or innovative lesson – and praise their efforts.

HIGH WILL/LOW SKILL:

High Will/Low Skill teachers tend to be the newer teachers in the building. Either they have recently graduated from a teacher preparation program or they have come to teaching because they want to make a difference and have taken an alternative certification route. They are excited about teaching and sincerely want to do what is best for their students, but they lack the pedagogical and/or the content area knowledge they need to be effective in the classroom.

The good news is these teachers are willing to learn. They just need to be pointed in the right direction. Often, they lack experience in the classroom and therefore struggle with classroom management.

The danger with High Will/Low Skill teachers is that their lofty ideals will sometime lead them to implement strategies that seem to make sense but which actually do students more harm than good. So eager are they to be effective in the classroom that they may try a variety of strategies or activities without giving much thought to whether these strategies or activities actually improve student achievement.

High Will/Low Skill teachers tend to struggle in three key areas: Lesson planning, classroom management, and content area knowledge.

High Will/Low Skill teachers SAY:

- I came across this great new strategy I am going to try.
- I love kids.
- I went into teaching for the intrinsic rewards.
- I have this terrific new activity I am going to use with my students.
- Nothing. When things aren't going well, it's hard for them to recognize or admit they need some help.

High Will/Low Skill teachers DO:

- Attend faculty meetings on time and participate enthusiastically.
- Tend to struggle with classroom management.
- Create lesson plans focused on activities versus mastery objectives.
- Tend to be very warm, friendly, and well-liked by students and parents.
- Create lessons lacking consistent rigor.
- Create lessons that may look good on paper but fail in execution.
- Invite you to their classrooms.
- Attend staff development training enthusiastically.
- Stay after school and during lunch to work with students.
- Have a hard time anticipating lesson elements that will confuse students.
- Allow students to pull them off track or engage in side discussions.
- Take feedback personally.

Strategies for High Will/Low Skill Teachers

- Share research and best practices focused on the particular instructional strategy or strategies that need to be addressed.
- Work with the teacher to develop specific improvement goals and steps in the improvement process.
- Celebrate progress towards goals.
- Use data to identify areas for improvement and to track progress.
- Build professional learning communities to provide support.
- Use informal observations as a way of providing quick feedback on progress towards goals.
- Provide clear, specific feedback in a structured but collegial context.
- Use exemplars and models of the teaching behaviors and strategies you expect to see.
- Establish clear benchmarks for improvement.
- Encourage suggestions and alternative ideas from the teacher.
- Provide opportunities for self-evaluation as skill set improves.
- Provide directives for improvement at first, but move to recommendations as skill set and knowledge base improves.
- Establish a formal support group facilitated by a master teacher that will allow teachers specific assistance through joint problem solving and an opportunity to learn and practice effective collegial interaction.
- Have teachers talk through a lesson step-by-step beforehand to learn to anticipate the times students will need support and clarification (for example, moving into groups, explaining multipart directions, distributing materials).
- Build a sense of control by providing written information experienced teachers take for granted – copies of the bell schedule, policies and procedures, contact people in the school for various needs.
- Arrange for the teacher to observe high will/high skill teachers in the building.

HIGH WILL/HIGH SKILL:

High Will/High Skill teachers are those teachers every leader dreams of having. Not only are they highly motivated and committed to their students' success, but they have the content knowledge and the pedagogical expertise that most likely results in student success. These are your master teachers.

The danger with High Skill/High Will teachers is that they are often neglected. We tend to spend the lion's share of our efforts with our ineffective teachers and leave the High Skill/High Will teachers to their own devices. If we are not careful, these teachers can reach professional ennui and just become plain bored. These teachers also can become genuinely overloaded as they are asked to take on more and more support for students and staff.

If that happens, we can quickly lose the teachers we most want to keep. They migrate to new schools or new positions in search of new challenges because we failed to provide them with the challenges that would keep them engaged and motivated to remain in our schools.

High Will/High Skill Teachers SAY:

- My principal never comes by my classroom.
- I can help any student learn.
- Yes, I'll help with the meeting, activity, field trip, conference, etc.

High Will/High Skill Teachers DO:

- Become frustrated with a lack of feedback from their instructional leader.
- Rarely receive visits to their classrooms.
- Mentor new and younger teachers.
- Are tapped by the district to write curriculum and conduct training.
- Will in engage in professional development but are careful about which activities they choose.
- Are cooperative during staff meetings but often get impatient with what they consider "fluff."
- Share their materials with other teachers.
- Have high expectations of students.
- Provide rigorous instruction.
- Have few classroom management issues.
- Rarely send students to the office.
- Hold students accountable for their behavior and their learning.
- Avoid the teachers lounge or other places where people complain.
- Express frustration with teachers who don't "get it".
- Wonder why they work so hard (especially if their efforts aren't acknowledged).
- Work independently for the good of the school and students.
- Make good decisions.
- Anticipate student confusion.

Strategies for High Will/High Skill Teachers

- Publicly recognize their accomplishments and have them share their learning with staff.

- Challenge them to increase their competence in a particular area.
- Actively seek their input in the day-to-day operations of the school.
- Provide them with informal leadership opportunities within the school
- Use informal observations as a way of providing acknowledgment for the work they do.
- Communicate that the work of excellent teachers is never done. Students' needs are constantly evolving and so should their practice.
- Provide opportunities for self-evaluation and reflection.
- Ask them to present their data to you and explain what the data indicates.
- Arrange for other teachers or other support professionals to provide some help (just because they planned the field trip doesn't mean they need to copy all the permission slips too).
- Help them develop leadership opportunities for developing teachers.

Collecting Data

In order to determine where each teacher is on the will/skill continuum, you will have to collect some data. There are two types of relevant data you will need to examine. The first is observational data and the second is student performance data.

OBSERVATIONAL DATA:

Observational data is information you collect by watching the teacher teach or interact with students, staff members, and parents. There are several tools you can use to collect this information.

Artifacts

Teacher and student artifacts can give you a good sense of both the teacher's will and skill. Examine lesson plans, assignment sheets, syllabi, written grading policies, student work, formal and informal assessment instruments, and rubrics to get a general sense of a teacher's instructional practice and priorities. Look at the lesson objectives and activities, how objectives and standards are communicated, the types of assignments students are given, the grading standards for the class, the amount and quality of student work, how students are assessed, the type of feedback the teacher provides, and whether the assignments, lessons, or units are tied to state and district standards.

In terms of teacher skill, artifacts will tell you how well teachers set and convey instructional objectives, how well they match the learning activities to these objectives, how well students are meeting these objectives, and how they will be able to tell whether students are meeting these objectives. The quality of these objectives, the fidelity to the district and state standards, their assessment criteria and priorities, the amount of support the artifacts provide students, and the teacher's response to students' work (i.e. grades, comments, and written grading policies) will give you clues about the teacher's will.

Walkthroughs

Although there are several types of walkthroughs, supervisory walkthroughs will best allow you to collect data for the purposes of designing a strategic conversation. These short classroom visits are conducted by a single instructional leader and are designed to gather a quick snapshot of individual classroom practice and offer specific, non-evaluative feedback as well as to develop a broader picture of classroom practice over time. You can focus on a specific department, grade level, subject, or teaching team. Plan to spend between 5 and 7 minutes in each classroom and visit a minimum of 3 classrooms at a time. Decide ahead of time what specific instructional behaviors you will be observing for and use a data collection tool to record your thoughts. (See the appendix for a walkthrough template and instructions)

Because of the short time you will be spending in the classroom, you will not be able to observe everything. Focus on one or two teaching skills across the classrooms you visit and look for how well a group of teachers applies those skills.

Walkthroughs can reveal teacher skill by helping you observe trends among teachers, trends with one specific teacher over time, or reveal very quickly how well a teacher or group of teachers is applying a specific skill. Look for specific teaching behaviors such as differentiated instructional strategies, effective communication of the lesson objective, student engagement, classroom management, levels of rigor, questioning strategies, use of explanatory devices, etc.

Walkthroughs reveal teacher will by showing you whether a teacher is responding to the feedback you are giving them as revealed by their instructional practice. Because walkthroughs allow you to make frequent trips into a classroom, you can gauge whether a teacher is actually making improvements and applying the feedback you have given to improve his practice.

Informal Observations

Informal observations are short, unannounced visits to individual classrooms designed to gather formative data on a teacher's instructional practice. They allow instructional leaders a series of snapshots of a teacher's instructional practice over time and provide you with several opportunities to give teachers feedback they can use to improve their instructional practice without the high-stakes environment of a formal observation.

Plan to spend 8-15 minutes in a classroom and observe for overall instructional strategies. Watch both the teachers' behavior and the students' behavior. In particular, pay attention to whether or not the objective of the instruction is clear to you and to the students. Because you are only in the classroom for a short time and because informal observations are designed to provide teachers with formative feedback on their instruction, only record observable behaviors on whatever observation format you are using. Write down what you see going on rather than what you think is going on or your assessments of what is taking place in the classroom. Share this data with teachers as a starting point for a reflective, facilitative, coaching, or directive conversation. (See the appendix for two different informational observation templates).

Informal observations will reveal skill because they will allow you to observe first-hand a teacher's ability to manage a classroom, organize a lesson around an objective, work effectively and efficiently towards achieving the learning objective, design learning experiences that move students towards the objective, respond to student questions, create a positive learning environment, pace the lesson, provision effectively, transition between one activity and the next, use a repertoire of explanatory and assessment strategies, and differentiate their instruction to respond to individual students' needs.

Informal observations will reveal a teacher's will by showing you how teachers respond to student questions, whether teachers attempt to engage all students, whether the teacher has made differentiated pathways to success for students, whether the teacher seems to have established supportive and caring relationships with students, and whether teachers communicate high expectations to students.

Formal Observations

Formal observations are longer classroom visits conducted by a single instructional leader to get a more comprehensive picture of a teacher's instructional practice. Plan to spend no less than 30 minutes and up to the entire class period observing a teacher's lesson. You then follow up with the teacher in a post-observation conference to share feedback, make recommendations, and provide an overall written summary and in some cases evaluation of what you observed.

Because these observations are directly tied to a teacher's evaluation, they tend to be threatening to teachers, especially when teachers are not clear about the process. Therefore, it is important that your process be transparent and that you build trust through the other observational strategies first. Use the formal observation process approved by your school district not only as a means of providing a final evaluation to teachers but as a way to help teachers make the connection between their instructional practices and student achievement. Use the post-observation conference to engage teachers in reflective, facilitative, coaching, or directive conversations around specific instructional behaviors and long-term professional development goals. (See the appendix for strategies for more effective formal observations and follow-up conferences).

The formal observation process will give you a more comprehensive look at a teacher's skill set. You will see a larger portion of the lesson so you can determine how a teacher prepares students for learning, establishes and communicates the lesson objective, introduces the material, explains the concepts, designs learning activities to help students meet the objective, responds to students' individual learning needs, paces the lesson, collects formative data on student progress, adjusts the lesson based on this data, and summarizes the content and provides lesson closure. During the post observation conference, you can further determine teacher skill by how teachers explain the instructional choices they made during the planning and implementation of the lesson and their assessment of how successful the lesson was.

The post-observation conference is also a powerful indicator of teacher will. How does the teacher talk about his/her students? How does the teacher explain students' success or failure in the classroom? Does the

teacher take ownership over his/her students' achievement? How does the teacher respond to feedback? Does the teacher actively participate in the conversation contributing not only to identifying areas of growth but also looking for solutions and suggesting professional development activities to further hone their teaching craft? How a teacher participates in the follow up discussion and responds to evaluative feedback will tell you whether the teacher has the will to improve his/her practice.

STUDENT PERFORMANCE DATA:
The ultimate measure of a teacher's instructional effectiveness is how well students master the objectives of the teacher's course. Thus, it is important to examine with teachers their students' performance. This data will guide the direction and content of your instructional feedback to teachers.

Formative Assessment Data

Formative assessments help teachers check student understanding in real time and allow teachers to opportunity to adjust their instruction to ensure all students meet the standard prior to the formal summative assessment. Take a look at whether teachers use formative assessments, the types of informal assessments they use, how they respond to the data revealed by the formative assessments, and whether students are showing progress towards mastery over a series of assessments over time.

Formative assessments reveal teacher skill by showing you how well the students are mastering the standards, whether the teacher has a clear goal for assessment, how well the teacher can analyze data to select the appropriate instructional response, the range and types of informal assessments the teacher uses, whether the assessment method teachers select is appropriate given the learning outcomes the teacher is trying to assess, and how well teachers are able to use informal assessments to diagnose where students are.

Formative assessments reveal teachers will by showing you how willing teachers are to respond to the data revealed by the assessment, and whether all students' scores garner the same response from the teacher. Does the teacher intervene for some students and not others? Do the assessments reveal that certain students or groups of students' needs are not being served? Is the teacher willing to adjust his/her instruction based on the assessment data? Does the teacher move on regardless of what the data reveals?

Student Grades

Take a good look at teachers' grades. Examine the number and types of assignments students are receiving, how assignments are graded, the weight different types of assignments are given, how many students are completing the assignments, the grading scale they are using, grading patterns, and grade distributions by assignment, unit, and grading period.

You can collect this data in several ways. Globally, you can look at student report card data and quickly assess the grade distribution for the marking period by teacher. If you put the data into a spreadsheet, you can take a look at the grade distribution by teacher, department, subject, grade level, or class.

You can also examine teacher's gradebooks, but be careful how you engage in this process. Demanding that teachers turn in their gradebooks periodically will just create panic and put teachers on the defensive. A better approach would be to invite teachers to come in and meet with you for five-ten minutes to discuss their gradebooks each quarter or semester. Tell teachers that you want to get a sense of how their students are doing and better understand their grading practices and approach. Invite teachers to show you their gradebooks and discuss their grading practices and their students' progress during the meeting. Ask questions to help you understand their thinking rather than making judgments or providing prescriptions. Remember, the purpose is to collect data. Once you have the data, you can plan a more comprehensive approach to address any concerns that may be raised while examining the gradebook.

Looking at students' grades will reveal teacher skill by showing you how well students are mastering the objectives of the unit. It will also show you whether or not teachers understand the purpose of grading, have a clear and reasonable grading approach, and have appropriately matched their grading practices to their subject and students. Students' grades will also expose teacher will by revealing whether or not teachers have a fair grading policy, whether teachers are consistently applying their grading policy, whether grades are being inflated or deflated, grade inequities or disparities for certain groups of students, and whether teachers are allowing certain students to fail.

Summative Assessment Data

Summative assessments are usually given at the end of a unit of study or the end of a course but they are also the state-mandated and national norm-referenced tests students encounter once a year. Summative assessments are based on a set of standards and tell you which students have mastered the standards, and which standards they mastered. Summative assessment data is fairly easy to collect. Take a look at final exam scores or state and national test scores and look for trends.

Summative assessments reveal teacher skill by telling you how many students have mastered the standards. Also, look at how teachers analyze their data and what observations they offer. This will tell you whether teachers are proficient at examining data and using data to identify areas for improvement, set goals, and improve their instructional practice.

You can get clues to teacher will by paying attention to how teachers respond

General Questions to Ask Using Data

BASED ON THESE DATA...

- whose needs does your class best serve?
- is there a pattern here?
- is student achievement predictable by some factor or combination of demographic factors such as race, gender, socio-economic status, ESOL or ESL status, etc.
- under what conditions are students most successful?
- what is the direct impact of that strategy on student performance?
- what changes (if any) do you need to make in your practice?
- what strategies seem to be working?
- does that strategy work for every student in your class?
- is there congruency between your expectations and student outcomes?
- what parts of the picture are still missing?
- what other data would make this picture more clear?
- what did students learn and what do they still need to learn?
- what other questions do these data raise?

to the summative data. Do they spend time looking for areas of improvement? Do they make excuses for their data or dismiss it out of hand? Are they willing to take ownership of their data or do they blame the students? Do they use the data to look for way they can improve? Are they willing to engage in discussions about data?

Remember, no one piece of data will be able to tell you everything. You need to use multiple data sources over time. Use the principle of triangulation as your guide and examine at least three data sources before you draw any conclusions about a teacher's will and skill. Even then, continue to collect and examine other data to confirm and refine your assessment.

NOW WHAT?

Once you have a sense of a teacher's will and skill, it is a lot easier to plan a series of strategic conversations that will address the teacher's individual needs. The next chapter will introduce you to the four types of strategic conversations and show you how to use each one with each of the four types of teachers.

Think About:

1. *What type of teacher were you before you became an instructional leader? Were you always that type of teacher? What experiences helped you become that type of teacher?*
2. *What type of teacher seems to be the most prominent type in your building? What type of teacher receives the most attention? Are there things in your institutional practice that encourage or discourage certain types of teachers to flourish and others to languish?*
3. *Why types of data do you typically collect? What types of data do you avoid collecting? Why?*
4. *How often do you share and discuss data with your staff? What opportunities do your staff have to respond or collect and share data of their own?*
5. *What data do you need to examine to determine what types of teaches are on your staff? What data do you have already and what data will you need to collect?*

Return to the four teachers in the introduction. Based on what you have just learned, answer the following questions:

6. *Which of the four types of teachers is Mrs. Henderson? What data questions might you ask during the post observation conference to help her examine her own data?*
7. *Which of the four types of teachers is Mr. Locke? What initial strategies would you use to work with him?*
8. *Which of the four types of teachers is Ms. Paulson? What three types of data would you collect to help you diagnose where she needs to improve?*
9. *Which of the four types of teachers is Mr. Terrell? What strategies would not work with him?*

MATCH THE NEEDS OF YOUR STAFF WITH THE APPROPRIATE CONVERSATIONAL APPROACH

Now that you have diagnosed who your teachers are, the next step is to match the appropriate conversational approach to each teacher's needs. There are four types of conversations you can use:

Reflecting involves helping teachers think intentionally about their instruction and drawing their own conclusions. When you are reflecting with teachers, you provide a safe environment where they can identify their instructional challenges, develop a plan of action, and decide what supports they will need. Your role is to ask reflective questions that help them look for commonalities, patterns, differences, and interrelations in their teaching attitudes and behaviors.

The goal of reflecting is to help teachers make connections between their behavior or attitudes and student achievement.

Facilitating involves taking a more active role in the conversation in order to help teachers clarify their thinking about their instructional practice. When you are facilitating, you help teachers identify the instructional challenge, develop an action plan, and identify the supports they will need. Your role is to ask strategic questions that help teachers: think more deeply about their practice, clarify their goals, identify the impact of their behavior on student achievement, unearth any misconceptions they may have, consider different points of view, and develop a plan of action. The goal of facilitating is to help teachers make commitments to improve their instructional practice in ways that will improve student achievement.

Coaching requires even more involvement from the instructional leader. When you are coaching, you are collaboratively working with teachers to identify the instructional challenge, develop an action plan, and provide feedback on their progress. Your role is to engage teachers in conversations that help them identify areas where they can grow, understand the root causes of their instructional challenges, learn the steps they need to take in order to improve, develop fluency in key teaching skills, and expand their awareness of available resources. The goal of coaching is to help teachers make corrections to their teaching behaviors so they can improve student achievement.

Directing is the most active leadership approach. It is also the least collaborative. When you are directing, you identify the instructional challenge, you develop the action plan, and you provide very specific feedback on the teacher's progress towards the goals you have identified. Your role is to name the teaching behavior that is presenting the challenge, describe its instructional impact, request the change in behavior, check for understanding, provide specific feedback, and implement positive or negative consequences. The goal of directing is to help teachers make changes in their teaching behavior so they can improve student achievement.

Remember, no one conversational approach will help you reach your goals with each teacher. It is the combination of all four approaches matched to the needs of each teacher and used judiciously over time that will help you help teachers improve. In this chapter, you will learn how to apply each of the four types of conversations and the outcomes you are likely to get when you apply them with each type of teachers. This will help you match the approach appropriately to where teachers are and what they need. In the next chapter, you will learn how to combine all four conversations to create a long-term approach for the teachers you serve.

Reflecting

Reflecting is the least intrusive of the strategic conversational approaches but it is often the most difficult to do. That is because as a profession, many of us are not used to spending time reflecting on our practice and it may feel a little unnatural or awkward at first.

Although every conversation you have with teachers should involve some degree of reflection, usually that reflection is a means to some other end. In the reflective conversation, reflection is an end in and of itself.

As an instructional leader, you can use reflection to help teachers make inferences, analyze the effect of their teaching behavior on students, evaluate the appropriateness of teaching strategies, discover alternate strategies, become more open to new ideas and approaches, analyze their own decision making, weigh competing points of view, and examine their own personal goals.

The power of reflecting is that it helps teachers learn from themselves. As the instructional leader, your role is to provide a safe environment where this self revelation can take place. By asking reflective questions you help teachers examine their actions, ideas, and beliefs. By, using reflective listening skills and summarizing, you help teachers distance themselves from their actions, ideas, and beliefs so they can scrutinize these more objectively. In the end, teachers draw their own conclusions about their behavior and make their own decisions about how they will behave in the future.

REFLECTING STRATEGIES

Reflecting with staff involves three strategies: Asking **reflective questions**, **reflective listening**, and **summarizing**.

The goal of **reflective questions** is to help teachers think intentionally about their instructional practice and the impact it has on students. Reflective questions ask teachers to consider what they did, how it affected students, what worked and did not work, and what steps they will take to improve. Reflective questions typically begin with *why* or *how*.

Reflective Listening involves two skills: Asking Follow-Up Questions and Paraphrasing. As you ask reflective questions, you should be listening for opportunities to ask follow up questions. Follow up questions should not be leading. Instead, they should help clarify teachers' thinking on a topic and help teachers to probe their answers more deeply. Some examples of follow up questions include:

- Why do you think that?
- How do you know that?
- What leads you to believe that?
- That's interesting. Tell me more.

Paraphrasing involves listening for key words or ideas, putting them in your own words, and then restating them to the listener.

Examples of Reflective Questions

- Why did you make that instructional decision?
- What was the impact of that decision on the students?
- Which students were most impacted by that decision and how?
- How do you know the students are learning?
- How does this lesson connect to other lessons in this unit?
- How will you know that students have mastered the objectives?
- How do you make decisions about what you will and will not teach?
- How could you improve the lesson next time?
- How did you last formative assessment measure affect this lesson?
- Who is the primary audience for this lesson?
- What was the single most important concept and skill you wanted every single child to know at the end of this lesson? How successful were you?
- Generally, how prepared were your students to receive this lesson prior to the start of class? What do you believe they already knew? What do you believe they did not know? How could you tell?
- Whose needs does your class best serve?
- How do your beliefs influence the way that you teach? How do your beliefs influence the way that you perceive students?
- What are the underlying assumptions that are revealed by that particular policy or approach?

You can use paraphrasing to communicate that you understood what the teacher was saying. If, in the process of paraphrasing, you misstate something the teacher has said, the teacher has the chance to clarify his or her point.

Also, paraphrasing helps teachers hear what they are saying. Sometimes, hearing their ideas reflected to them, will often spark even greater reflection as they elaborate on what they were saying. Some examples of paraphrasing include:

- What I hear you saying is...
- I thought I heard you say that...
- So what you are saying is...

Summarizing:

At the end of the reflective conversation, it is helpful to summarize the main points and discuss how what was learned during the reflective process will ultimately impact the teacher's future instructional practice.

During the discussion, listen for key points. When you are wrapping up the discussion, summarize these key points and then ask:

- How will this impact what you do in the future?
- What do you think this will mean to the way you plan in the future?
- Now that you have realized ___, what will you do about it?

By summarizing the conversation, you can help the teachers identify what they learned and plan for how they will use what they have learned in their future practice.

Blase & Blase (2004) offer a few other caveats for reflection:

- Reflection is a shared learning experience where both the teacher and the instructional leader use their collective expertise.
- Reflective conversations require protected time.
- A lack of trust will preclude effective reflection.
- The ability to reflect must be developed over time.
- Developing effective reflection requires verbal support and modeling on behalf of the instructional leader.

REFLECTING AND THE FOUR TYPES OF TEACHERS

There are three factors that affect a teacher's ability to reflect. The first and most important factor is the teacher's motivation to reflect and learn from the reflective conversation. If a teacher is not motivated to reflect, then the quality of the reflection is significantly reduced. Therefore, it is often difficult to use a reflective conversation with a low will teacher.

A teacher's ability to reflect on a topic is also directly proportional to the teacher's understanding of the topic. Therefore, teachers who do not have a great deal of content or pedagogical knowledge will not be as reflective as a teacher who does. This means it may be difficult to hold a reflective conversation with a low skill teacher.

While the first two factors have to do with the characteristics of the teacher, the third factor has to do with your own ability to establish trust and rapport with teachers. That is because the third factor affecting a teacher's ability to reflect is their confidence in the person with whom they are reflecting. If they do not feel safe, if they do not believe the conversation is confidential and that it will not be used against them, teachers cannot reflect effectively.

Based on these three factors, reflecting works best with High Will/High Skill teachers and is least effective with Low Will/Low Skill teachers. That does not mean you cannot use reflective conversations with all teachers, but it does mean you will have to carefully plan how you will reflect with them in order to be effective.

High Will/High Skill teachers really benefit from reflective conversations because it allows them to probe their practice more

deeply. Because they are highly motivated, they will enjoy engaging in reflection and will often reflect on their own. And, because they are highly skilled, they will be able apply what they learn from their reflection to their practice.

With **Low Will/High Skill**, reflection is a good tool to use to help them begin to examine the impact of their own teaching behavior on their students' achievement. Low Will/High Skill teachers have the content and pedagogical knowledge they need in order to be reflective but lack the motivation to engage in such conversations. For these teachers, it is best to build reflection into the casual conversations you have with them as you stop and chat with them in the halls. Ask them how things are going and listen for opportunities to ask follow up questions. Then paraphrase their answers and ask more follow up questions. Gently challenge any erroneous assumptions you see emerge in the conversation and then ask a follow up question that will help the teacher consider an alternate point of view.

Use reflective conversations with **High Will/Low Skill** teachers to help them uncover what they still need to learn to be more effective teachers. High Will/Low Skill teachers may be motivated to have reflective conversations, but because they lack the content and pedagogical knowledge, they often don't know how to make connections between their own actions and their students' achievement. Therefore, it is important that as you paraphrase, you help them make the connections. Your follow up questions should help them recognize what it is they still don't know and to think about what steps they will take to acquire this knowledge.

The purpose of reflecting with **Low Will/ Low Skill** teachers is to help them to begin to think about their teaching practice. Low Will/ Low Skill teachers can engage in reflective conversations but instructional leaders have to be careful to prime these teachers for reflection. The first step is to create a safe environment. That means it is probably better not to call the teacher into your office and announce "We are now going to have a reflective conversation." Instead, make the conversation informal and work it into the course of a conversation you are already having with the teacher.

Begin by asking the teacher to react to a specific event. This event does not have to be a teaching event that occurred in the classroom. It could be another event such as something the two of you observed together or something that happened to someone else. The goal is to get the teacher to share how they feel about the event.

Once the teacher has shared how they feel about the event, the next step is to get the teacher to elaborate on their feelings by comparing the event to an experience they may have had. You can also ask them to compare the event to a theory or a moral or philosophical position they may hold.

Finally, ask the teacher to think about how this event might impact their own teaching practice. Be warned, this step can be difficult for the Low Will/Low Skill teacher and many teachers will not reach this stage of the conversation at first. That's okay. If you can get the teacher to at least begin reflecting by getting to stage two of this process, you have made progress. Continue to engage these teachers in these kinds of conversations from time to time until they become used to thinking about events or issues on this level. In time, the teacher will become more reflective.

SUMMARY:

Who?

- Low will/low skill
- Low will/high skill
- High will/low skill
- High will/high skill

What Tools?

- Ask reflective questions
- Ask follow up questions
- Paraphrasing
- Summarizing

When?

- When teachers need help thinking objectively about their practice.

Where?

- Teacher's classroom
- Hallway
- Conference table

Why?

- To help teachers make connections between their own behavior and its impact on student achievement.

Think About:

1. *How would Ms. Henderson react to a reflective conversation? How would you need to structure a reflective conversation with Ms. Henderson so that it would be effective in helping her improve her instructional practice?*
2. *Why would you use a reflective conversation with Mr. Locke? What would you need to do in the conversation to help Mr. Locke reflect about his practice?*
3. *What would you have to do first to help Ms. Paulson effectively engage in a reflective conversation? What reflective questions would you use to uncover the reasons for her resistance?*
4. *How can a reflective conversation help Mr. Terrell remain challenged and motivated? What types of questions would you need to ask?*
5. *How can you use reflecting to help the teachers you lead?*
6. *With which teachers do you need to reflect? How will you structure those conversations?*
7. *Which of the reflecting skills will you need to develop in order to better help teachers reflect on their practice?*
8. *How often and how well do you reflect on your own practice?*

Facilitating

Facilitative conversations allow you to talk with teachers about their own data and then mediate the teacher's assessment of what the data means and what he should do about it.

In facilitative conversations, you remain mostly neutral. You want to let the teacher take the lead, but facilitating does involve some guidance from you. When you facilitate, you are guiding teachers towards a particular outcome; however, the teacher has an active role in selecting the pathway to that outcome. The leader sets the outcome and the instructional leader helps the teacher reach the outcome.

Facilitating is collaborative. Your job as a facilitator is to prompt deeper inquiry into an instructional challenge and to collaboratively come up with a course of action. You help teachers maintain a focus on the goal and help them access the resources they need. The teacher identifies the instructional challenge and then you help facilitate the process they use to meet resolve it. The teacher sets the goal (often after reflection) and you help them reach their goal by suggesting resources, helping them gain access to the supports they need, making suggestions regarding a plan of action, and providing feedback.

TIPS FOR EFFECTIVE FACILITATION:

- Listen first before making suggestions.
- Make suggestions in such a way as to extend, broaden, or enrich teachers' thinking and strengths.
- When making suggestions, share your own professional experiences to encourage teacher reflection.
- When making suggestions about improving teaching, use examples and demonstrations.
- Give teachers discretion or choice to accept or reject your suggestions.
- Make suggestions that are in the best interest of students regardless of what the current district policy advocates.
- Encourage teachers to take risks
- Support suggestions by providing supplementary materials.
- Make suggestions face-to-face
- Focus on effective instructional methods and current educational research.

In a facilitative conversation you will also work with teachers to identify obstacles to their success. You then work to remove these obstacles or at least mitigate them so that teachers are more likely to be successful. You might change their schedule for instance so that they can plan with their colleagues, or reduce the number of classes they teach or change their responsibilities so that they can focus on developing their skill set in one area.

In a facilitative conversation, one of your main roles is to make suggestions. You will provide teachers with ideas they can use to improve their practice. A teacher will accept or reject a suggestion based on two factors. First, the teacher has to see a fit between the suggestion and the students' needs. It is your job in a facilitative conversation to use data so that you both have a clear picture of students' needs. Then you can make suggestions based on what the data is telling you and are therefore more likely to directly connect your suggestions to students' needs.

Second, the teacher has to feel that they have the ability to perform or enact the suggestion. Be careful not to make suggestions that go too far beyond the teacher's skill set. And, as you make suggestions include supports to help teachers apply those suggestions to their practice.

FACILITATION AND THE FOUR TYPES OF TEACHERS

Because the goal of facilitation is to help teachers clarify their thinking about their instructional practice and to make specific commitments to improve, a teacher's ability to engage in a facilitative conversation will be impacted more heavily by their will than their skill. Low will teachers will have more trouble making commitments than high will teachers.

For the **low will/low skill** teacher, facilitation is best only after you have begun working with this teacher. It is not good to start with a facilitative conversation. First you must work on helping low will/low skill teachers develop more will. Only after you have been working with this teacher for a while should you begin facilitation. In fact, the goal of your initial work with low will/low skill teachers will be to move them towards a more facilitative relationship.

Once you have begun to impact their will, you can use the facilitative conversation to help low will/low skill teachers begin to acquire the supports and skills they need in order to improve their instructional practice. As these teachers move towards either increased will or increased skill and begin to migrate into the other quadrants, you can use the facilitative conversation more.

When working with **low will/high skill** teachers, you can use the facilitative conversation to help them develop or refine a specific teaching skill. Because these teachers are low will, they may not easily recognize or own their instructional challenges. Thus, it is important to begin the facilitative conversation by examining data. Your job at the beginning of the conversation is to discuss the data and to mediate the teacher's assessment of what the data means. Once you have used the data to help the low will/high skill teacher recognize that they do have an instructional challenge, you can move to a facilitative conversation designed to help them resolve their instructional challenge.

In both cases it is important to allow low will/high skill teachers to arrive at their own conclusions both about what the data means and about what decisions or direction they need to take in response to the data. Your job is to facilitate their analysis and decision making by asking reflective questions, summarizing their responses, prompting them to make a commitment about their next steps, and providing structures that will help them be accountable to their commitments.

For **high will/low skill** teachers, the facilitative conversation is best used as a way to transition them from a coaching relationship towards a more autonomy. As these teachers increase their skill level, use the facilitative conversation to prompt them to look critically at their practice, diagnose their own teaching challenges, and make their own decisions about what they should do next. In the beginning high will/low will skill teachers may be able to identify their instructional challenge but will need help from you discovering the root cause and brainstorming possible solutions. Resist the urge to determine these for the teacher. Instead, use reflective questions to help the teacher discover the root cause. Use brainstorming activities to help the teacher identify possible solutions. You can help teacher weigh the pros and cons of each solution but leave the final decision to the teacher. Allow these teachers to identify what supports they will need and encourage them to look outside of you for those supports. High will/low skill teachers will also need more follow up after a facilitative conversation to track their progress and provide useful feedback they can use to improve.

High will/high skill teachers may need facilitation from time to time when, through reflection, they realize they need to improve their skill set in a particular area. Facilitative conversations can also be useful to help high will/high skill teachers commit to expanding their repertoire of skills. Allow these teachers a considerable amount of autonomy both in identifying their challenges and in brainstorming solutions. Your role here is to contribute ideas about possible resources the teacher hadn't considered or did not realize were available. You also want to help high will/high skill teachers develop strategies to hold themselves accountable to any commitments they make and to track their progress. Set a time to have a follow up conversation and allow them to report on their progress to you. Use this follow up conversation as an opportunity to encourage and praise high will/high skill teachers in order to keep them motivated to improve.

SUMMARY:

Who?

- Low will/low skill
- Low will/high skill
- High will/low skill
- High will/high skill

What Tool?

- Facilitative Conversation
- Action Planning

When?

- When teachers need support to accomplish goals they have selected.

Where?

- Media center

- Teacher's classroom
- Your office conference table

Why?

- To help teachers make commitments to resolve instructional challenges.

Think About:

1. *What data would you use to begin a facilitative conversation with Mrs. Henderson? What suggestions would you make to Mrs. Henderson based on these data? What other steps would you have to take with Mrs. Henderson in order for her to respond positively to your suggestions?*
2. *What obstacles might you uncover during a facilitative conversation with Mr. Locke? What strategies would you use to help him overcome these obstacles?*
3. *What challenges will you face when having a facilitative conversation with Ms. Paulson? What steps would you have to take to help Ms. Paulson engage in a facilitative conversation?*
4. *Under what circumstances would you use a facilitative conversation with Mr. Terrell?*
5. *What steps will you need to take before you can effectively engage the teachers on your staff in facilitative conversations?*
6. *With which staff members might a facilitative conversation be most effective?*
7. *What kind of follow up might a facilitative conversation require?*

The Facilitative Conversation Worksheet

The goal of the facilitative conversation is to help the teacher think through an instructional challenge and with your help, develop possible solutions and a plan of action. Work through the following worksheet with teachers to help them systematically think through an instructional challenge.

ISSUE: What specific instructional issue do you want to address?	
ROOT: What do you think is at the root of this instructional issue?	
IDEAL STATE: What is the ideal state? What would instruction look like in this teacher's classroom if this issue was resolved?	
SOLUTION: How can the teacher resolve the issue and achieve the ideal state? What specific steps should he/she take?	
SUPPORTS: What supports will the teacher need in order to take these steps?	
PROGRESS: How will you track the teacher's progress towards achieving this goal? When will you know that the teacher has achieved the ideal state?	

Coaching

Coaching conversations occur when an instructional leader along with a teacher identifies an area of need and the instructional leader helps the teacher improve in that area by making recommendations and collaboratively developing an action plan. The goal of coaching is to provide growth-oriented feedback to teachers that will help them make changes to improve their instructional practice.

Coaching is different from reflecting or facilitating. While the first two are more concerned with thinking through the impact of specific teaching behaviors and resolving specific instructional challenges, coaching is more concerned with increasing capacity and developing or refining certain teaching skills. Thus, coaching is less concerned with specific behaviors or classroom occurrences and more concerned with developing a skill

THE SIX STEPS TO COACHING:

1. Describe the behavior or skill you are addressing as specifically as possible. What skill or behavior needs improving?
2. Discuss the impact of the behavior or skill. Show how the current behavior or skill area affects students and their learning. Discuss the consequences to students if the behavior or skill deficit continues. Solicit the teacher's opinion and listen for clues about what may be causing the behavior. Solicit his/her input on the impact the behavior may be having on students.
3. Make a recommendation about how the teacher can improve his/her behavior or improve the skill you are addressing. Again, solicit suggestions from the teacher as well.
4. Decide together on the goals for improvement.
5. Build agreement on the next steps. Work with the teacher to decide what the next steps should be. What specific steps should the teacher take to improve? Develop an action plan that includes how you will know when the skill or behavior has improved. What metrics will you include?
6. Follow up and provide feedback. Set specific times when you will follow up either through direct observation or through a follow up conversation. During the follow up conversation, discuss the action plan and provide specific feedback on where the teacher is in relation to the goals.

set that will be used to develop a range of teaching behaviors or deal with a variety of instructional challenges.

As the instructional leader, you will take a more active role in coaching than you will in facilitating or reflecting in that you will be making recommendations rather than suggestions. There is a difference.

A suggestion is optional; teachers can implement suggestions if they want. Suggestions imply that their present performance is okay, and there is no real damage to students if they continue. A recommendation signals that the teacher must change what he/she is doing and the instructional leader will follow up to be sure. *How* the change is made is up for discussion and the teacher can choose, but that the teacher must change is not optional.

Unlike a facilitative conversation where the teacher identifies the challenge and determines the next steps, a coaching conversation will require you to identify the teaching challenge and make a recommendation about what changes need to be made. Then together, you and the teacher can decide how to act on your recommendation. Be careful to recommend steps that will have a direct impact on the teacher's behavior.

Because recommendations requires that a teacher change his/her behavior, you should attach a timeline to any recommendation that you make. Give the teacher a few weeks to practice implementing the new behavior. Then, set a deadline for when the teacher will be expected to consistently implement the new behavior in the classroom. After that deadline, the teacher should be help accountable for implementing that behavior.

Implied in a coaching relationship is that you are an expert in a particular instructional area. Thus it is important that you remain abreast of the latest educational research and that you work to be seen as not just an instructional leader, but an effective practitioner yourself. You can accomplish this by teaching model lessons from time to time, sharing articles with teachers, writing articles yourself, discussing various instructional approaches with teachers, and demonstrating instructional strategies.

Because coaching is more hands on than both reflecting and facilitating, there are a range of strategies you can employ. You can provide teachers with professional learning opportunities designed to help develop their understanding of the content, facilitate study groups, co-teach with teachers, take teachers on collegial walkthroughs and then debrief about what they observed, provide non-evaluative classroom observations to look for the development of a specific skill, host reading groups to discuss relevant educational research or a useful educational book, or meet with teachers individually or in teams to help design more effective units or assessments, or examine student data together.

As a coach, your interactions with teachers should help teachers critically examine their practice, develop solutions to their teaching challenges, take appropriate risks, and access helpful resources. You can use the coaching relationship to encourage teachers and to build their confidence by helping them see how their progress directly impacts student learning.

A coaching relationship requires a certain degree of trust and safety in order for it to be effective. Because you will be actively involved in providing feedback to teachers, you will have to work to ensure that teachers do not see your feedback as evaluative or threatening. If they do, then any changes they make in their behavior will not be intrinsically motivated and will probably not last.

TIPS FOR EFFECTIVE COACHING

- Share literature especially about current trends and issues
- Allow space and time to practice new skills
- Demonstrate or model new skills (or find someone who can)
- Use peers to provide additional coaching
- Use action research
- After sharing resources, invite teachers to discuss them
- Provide time for group planning and collaboration
- Provide release time for peer coaching, observing, and collegial walk-throughs

COACHING AND THE FOUR TYPES OF TEACHERS

Low will/low skill teachers often resist coaching relationships at first because they require a high degree of interaction with the instructional leader. These teachers may prefer to be told what to do rather than interact and brainstorm solutions together. Additionally, low will/low skill teachers may regard your initial attempts at coaching with suspicion because many of their prior interactions with their instructional leaders have been evaluative in nature.

But, after you have worked with low will/low skill teachers for a while and developed a degree of trust and rapport both through reflective conversations, you can begin to support low will/low skill teachers by developing a coaching relationship. The key is to first establish trust.

In order to help these teachers see you as a means of support rather than as an evaluator, your recommendations should be designed to help them develop a particular skill set rather than to address a specific or immediate problem (use a facilitative or directive conversation to deal with specific problems). Begin with skills that are relatively discrete and therefore easier to acquire (such as effective provisioning or wait time) and build towards more complex skills (such as pacing or anticipating confusion). Provide

plenty of encouragement and sincere praise and save coaching conversations only for situations where you believe these teachers are ready and willing to make improvements.

When providing low will/low skill teachers with feedback be very specific about what constitutes success. Because low will/low skill teachers are often reluctant to commit to changing, you will have to take a more active role in identifying what the recommended change will look like in the classroom. Being specific will help both you and teachers understand what it is you are asking them to do and how you both will know when the teacher has successfully made the change you have requested.

Establishing trust is also key to developing coaching relationships with **low will/high skill** teachers. Because these teachers often blame forces outside of themselves for difficulties in the classroom, they may not be as receptive to your recommendations. It is therefore important to begin coaching conversations by examining data. Sharing the data can help low will/high skill teachers understand why you are making a recommendation and the data may help them identify a reasonable solution. Keep the conversation focused on the impact on student achievement and try to tie any accountability measures you identify directly to student achievement. In this way, you will help keep the low will/high skill teacher focused on outcomes.

Because low will/high skill teachers already have a wide repertoire of teaching strategies and a depth of knowledge of their content, you can give them latitude in identifying possible steps in the action plan. This is also an opportunity to work with teachers' strengths and to build ownership of the problem. If teachers are actively involved in developing solutions they are less likely to see your recommendation as evaluative or directive.

The coaching conversation is particularly useful when working with **high will/low skill** teachers. Because they are still developing a skill set, they often lack the ability to identify their instructional challenges or develop solutions. High will/low skill teachers need your recommendations both to help them identify the cause of their instructional challenge and to determine possible solutions.

That does not mean the conversation cannot be collaborative. You will still need to solicit their input on what steps they should take in their action plan, but only after you have led them through an assessment of the situation and have helped them see the impact of their teaching behaviors on student achievement. Try to break action steps down into small parts and make them as concrete as possible.

Following up with high will/low skill teachers is important not just because such follow up holds them accountable, but because following up gives you an opportunity to provide feedback that will further facilitate their improvement. Thus, you may have to follow up more frequently with high will/low skill teachers both to offer feedback and to offer encouragement as they try new strategies and develop new skills.

Remind teachers that growth is often not linear so they may encounter set backs. Try to predict what set backs they may encounter so teachers are not discouraged when they happen. Allow teachers to make mistakes but be sure to help them reflect on their mistakes and to learn from them.

Your coaching relationship with high will/low skill teachers may be more intense at first, but as teachers develop more proficiency, encourage them to be more actively involved in the analysis and to brainstorm possible solutions. Provide liberal praise and encouragement throughout the process.

Although **high will/high skill** teachers rarely need coaching, there are times when coaching conversations can be beneficial especially as you encourage these teachers to stretch and expand their repertoire of skills. Often, after reflection high will/high skill teachers will identify an area of growth and need your feedback and active support as they try new strategies or learn new skills.

While you will still make recommendations, high will/high skill teachers may be more active in developing an action plan and identifying both next steps and appropriate metrics for success. In fact, they may come to you with a specific teaching challenge and a clearly defined sense of what the ideal state should be and simply need you to make recommendations on how they can best get there.

Feedback is important to the high will/high skill teacher, especially targeted praise, but you may need to provide feedback less often than you would with other teachers. Still, may high will/high skill teachers are eager to grow and improve their craft and will want your feedback as they make progress.

SUMMARY:

Who?

- Low will/low skill
- Low will/low skill
- Low will/high skill
- High will/low skill

What?

- Coaching Conversation
- Growth Oriented feedback
- Informal observations

When?

- When teachers need to develop new skills.

Where?

- Teacher's classroom.
- Your office conference table.

Why?

- To help teachers make corrections in their teaching skill set.

Think About:

1. *How would Mrs. Henderson respond to a coaching conversation? What will you need to do to prepare Mrs. Henderson for coaching?*
2. *What strategies would you need to use to help Mr. Locke benefit from a coaching conversation? What follow up would Mr. Locke need to ensure that he applies your recommendations?*
3. *Why would you use a coaching conversation with Ms. Paulson? Why might you avoid using a coaching conversation with Ms. Paulson?*
4. *How would you adjust a coaching conversation so that Mr. Terrell would benefit from it?*
5. *What teachers in your building would benefit from coaching conversations? What groundwork will you have to lie in order to help them get the most out of these conversations?*
6. *With what other conversations would you combine a coaching conversation to increase its benefit?*

9. *In what circumstances might a coaching conversation be inappropriate?*
10. *What is the primary difference between a suggestion and a recommendation and how do you determine which is most appropriate? How would you phrase a suggestion differently than you would a recommendation?*

The Coaching Conversation Worksheet

Use the following worksheet to plan your coaching conversations. Complete this worksheet before you engage in the conversation with teachers.

STEP ONE: Describe the Behavior or Skill you want to address.	
STEP TWO: What is the impact of this behavior or skill area on students?	
STEP THREE: What recommendations can you make to help improve in this area?	
STEP FOUR: What specific goals would you like to see towards improving in this area?	
STEP FIVE: What steps will the teacher need to make in order to achieve this goal?	
STEP SIX: How will you monitor this plan and follow up with the teacher?	

The Coaching Conversation Action Plan

Use this worksheet to develop an action plan with teachers based on your coaching conversation.

GOAL: What goal or goals have you identified?		
STEPS: What steps will you take towards achieving your goal?	**SUPPORTS:** What supports will you need in order to take each step?	**TIMELINE:** When will you start and complete each step?
DATA: What data will you collect to determine whether you have achieved your goal?		

Directing

Although reflecting, facilitating, and coaching are the preferred methods for helping teachers improve their instructional practice, there are times when these approaches are ineffective in helping teachers recognize the impact of their behavior on student achievement. Some teachers do not immediately demonstrate either the will or the skill to adjust their behavior in the best interests of their students. In these cases, you will need to take a more directive approach.

The purpose of the directive conversation is help teachers make an immediate change. You are not only providing directives for what change needs to be made and how it should be made, you are also providing conditions for success and accountability for action.

Directive conversations are the least interactive of the dynamic leadership approaches. When you are engaged in a directive conversation, you do not make suggestions or even recommendations because both leave the decision about what must be done to some degree up to the teacher. If you have reached the point of direction, you can no longer leave the decision up to the teacher. Instead, of a suggestion or a recommendation, you will need to communicate an expectation where you spell out that the teacher must change, what change the teacher must make, how the teacher will make the change, how the teacher will be held accountable for making the change .

Reflecting, facilitating, and coaching approaches allow teachers more participation in identifying and resolving instructional challenges. In the directive conversation, the instructional leader identifies the concern, shares an expectation for improvement, and outlines what steps they expect teachers to take in order to improve.

That does not mean there is not room for collaboration in a directive conversation however. As with all strategic conversational approaches, it is important to remain open to alternate points of view. The teacher may have a different assessment of the situation. You should not only solicit their input but remain open to adjust your expectations based on their input. In order to increase the likelihood that the teacher will follow your directive, it is imperative that the teacher make some choices. By soliciting their input and allowing them to make some choices you can help teachers move beyond superficial compliance towards sharing ownership of the problem.

Instructional leaders must be careful about using a directive conversation because it does shift the power dynamic. It is a more formal conversation and you are not giving teachers many options either on the assessment of the situation or on the steps you want them to take to resolve the situation. Therefore, it is important to use directive conversations only when there is an immediate threat to students' social, academic, or psychological

well being or if other approaches have failed.

In a directive conversation, you are taking on a more supervisory role and this may be uncomfortable both for you and for the teacher with whom you are working. To ease this discomfort and to make the conversation more productive, acknowledge the teacher's situation before you state your expectations. In that way, you let the teacher know you understand her situation and also short circuit any excuses the teacher may be prepared to make.

You should also maintain a focus on the data. It is easy to get sidetracked, especially with more resistant teachers. But, if you keep the focus on the data and if you are prepared with multiple sources of data, the teacher may not like what you are asking him to do, but it will be difficult to argue with it.

Finally, you should make your directives as specific as possible. Do not share "concerns" or "issues." Instead, focus on specific behaviors that directly impact student achievement. Clearly communicate that the teacher is underperforming in a particular area by emphasizing the gap between what the teacher is doing and the standard or the desired state. You may have a list of improvements you would like to see a teacher make, but focus your directive conversations on those behaviors that have the greatest impact on students. Address only one problem at a time and make sure your directives focus on measurable changes in behavior rather than on transforming the teacher in a short period of time.

There are five steps to providing direction effectively:

1. Be very specific about what it is you would like to see the teacher do. State what you want in one to three sentences.
2. Explain your rationale behind your direction. Be sure to include data to support your direction.
3. Check to ensure that the teacher understands what it is you are asking of him/her.
4. Ask the teacher if s/he has any questions or an alternate point of view.
5. Listen carefully and acknowledge any concerns.
6. Provide the necessary support the teacher may need in order to carry out your direction.

After you have a directive conversation, it is vital that you follow up with teachers to hold them accountable to the directive you have given. Much of the time this follow up will need to be in writing in the form of a memo of understanding. You will also need to maintain documentation on teachers' progress. These data will be vital in holding teachers accountable.

Your follow up should also include informal conversations that help teachers reflect on the impact their behavior has on student success. In fact, it is important that you engage the teacher in a reflective conversation within a few days following a directive conversation to give the teacher an opportunity to process your directive. This reflective conversation need not be long or even a formal conversation, but you should give the teacher an opportunity to react to your directive and make the connection between their teaching behavior and the impact on students for themselves. Once the teacher has made the connection, you can move to coaching or facilitating. Combining directive conversations with reflection and coaching will not only communicate to teachers that you share the responsibility for their success but it will help forge a more collaborative relationship where real and sustained improvement is more likely to occur.

DIRECTIVE CONVERSATIONS AND THE FOUR TYPES OF TEACHERS

Because directive conversations are designed to address a lack of will, they are most useful with low will teachers. **Low will/low skill** teachers in particular may need directives at the beginning of your work with them in order to help them make necessary changes immediately for the benefit of their students. Because these teachers lack both the will to change and the skill to make effective changes, they will require more direction from you. Keep in mind that these teachers have less insight into the root causes of the teaching problem, and are less capable of

TIPS FOR EFFECTIVE DIRECTIVE CONVERSATIONS

- Focus specifically on observed behavior. Do not make assumptions about motives or conjectures on what the teacher may have been thinking.
- Include an explanation for the directive.
- Be non-evaluative and non-judgmental (hold up a mirror).
- Be specific about the effect actions have on students.
- Express sincere caring, interest, and support.
- When identifying steps, be sure that each step moves teachers closer to solving the problem.
- Make directives specific enough that it is clear when they have been met and when they have not been met.
- The teacher should have the primary responsibility for implementing the action steps.
- Identify what data sources you will use to determine that the directive has been implemented.
- Focus your directives on measurable changes in behavior.
- Make yourself available to discuss your direction subsequent to the conference.

self-monitoring. Therefore, they may not be able to follow your direction without support and follow up from you.

Maintain a focus on specific behaviors and only address one behavior at a time. You may also need to break your directive down into discrete steps and provide a time line for each step. If a teacher does not have the skill set they need to follow your directive, provide the necessary support to increase the likelihood the directive will be followed.

Low will/high skill teachers have the skill to follow your directives typically but they lack the will to make change on their own. Begin your interaction by facilitating a commitment to change but if the teacher resists your suggestions or your recommendations, move to a more directive conversation. Keep accurate records of your earlier efforts and share this information with teachers as a way of explaining why you are taking a more directive approach. Then, return to the data that prompted your intervention and explicitly connect the behavior you are addressing to student achievement. By keeping a focus on the data, you can limit the inevitable denials and excuses.

One potential challenge with sharing directives with low will/high skill teachers is that many of these teachers have received favorable evaluations in the past. As a result, they may resist your directives because they have not been held accountable for making changes. This is another reason to keep the focus on the observable data and for using multiple data sources as a means of explaining your rationale for making the directive.

Because low will/high skill teachers are skilled in their content and pedagogy, you can invite their input on how they should act on your directive once you have secured agreement on the problem and its root causes. In some cases, these teachers will refuse to see the problem and may resist your intervention. Even when teachers refuse to cooperate, you must still share your expectations, build a plan and hold teachers accountable to the plan. You will document both the plan and the teacher's refusal to participate in building the plan and then provide highly structured follow up in the form of formal observations to make sure that the teacher is accountable for following your directive. (See the sample memorandum of understanding for an example of how you can document the directive conversation).

Directive conversations with **high will/ low skill** teachers rarely happen because these teachers are more open to suggestions and recommendations. Use directive conversations with high will/low skill teachers only in extreme cases where the teacher's behavior poses an immediate threat to the well-being of students. In other cases, use the coaching or facilitative conversation to help these teachers make changes in their behavior.

When you do need to use directive conversation with high will/low skill teachers, work to lessen the formality of the conversation lest you damage the relationship you have established. Spend most of your time clearly stating the problem and explaining your rationale for your directive. You may need to issue a directive to stop a behavior that threatens students' immediate well being and then shift the conversation to a coaching conversation where you help these teachers develop the necessary skills to replace the offending behavior with one that is much more conducive to student success.

You will almost never need to use a directive conversation with **high will/high skill** teachers. In the very extreme case where the teacher is doing something that poses an immediate threat to students' well being and all other approaches have failed, try to make the directive conversation as collaborative as possible. You are still responsible for identifying the problem but use reflection to help discover the root causes, and facilitation to collaboratively determine what steps need to be taken to improve.

SUMMARY:

Who?

- Low will/low skill
- Low will/high skill

What Tools?

- The directive conversation
- Data
- Follow up
- Evaluation

When?

- When teachers are doing something that is to the detriment of their students.

Where?

- Your office behind your desk.

Why?

- To help teachers change their behavior immediately.

Think About:

1. *What steps would you have to take to help Mrs. Henderson act on a directive conversation? How will she react to your directive and how will you need to follow up to ensure that your directive is followed?*
2. *Why might a directive conversation be appropriate for Mr. Locke? What follow up will you need to provide?*
3. *How might Ms. Paulson respond to a directive conversation? What will you have to do to ensure that Ms. Paulson follows your directive?*
4. *Under what circumstances would a directive conversation be appropriate for Mr. Terrell? How would you adjust the conversation for him?*
5. *Under what circumstances is a directive conversation appropriate? Under what circumstances might you use another conversational approach instead?*
6. *What is the difference between a suggestion, recommendation, and expectation? Under what circumstances is each appropriate?*
7. *Why is it necessary to follow up directive conversations with reflective conversations? Are there instances where this is not necessary?*
8. *Why is it important to document your directives?*

The Directive Conversation Worksheet

When planning a directive conversation, it is a good idea to map out your ideas ahead of time. Use the following worksheet to help you plan your directive conversation.

STEP ONE: What is it you want the teacher to do (or stop doing)?	
STEP TWO: What is your rationale for this directive? What data do you have to support this rationale?	
STEP THREE: How will you know that the teacher understands your directive?	
STEP FOUR AND FIVE: What questions or concerns might the teacher have? How will you address these?	
STEP SIX: What support will the teacher need to follow your directive?	
FOLLOW UP: How will you check to see that your directive was followed? What consequences will you implement if it has not been followed?	

Memorandum of Understanding Template

TO: Teacher
FROM: Instructional Leader
DATE: Date
RE: Follow up from our conversation dated ___________

DEAR MR. /MS. TEACHER:

Thank you for taking the time to meet with me today to discuss (*general statement of the problem*). The following is a summary of our conversation:

- ____________________ (Specific statement of the problem)
- ____________________ (Data to support your assessment of the problem)
- ____________________ (Directive)

In the course of our conversation, I committed to (*outline the support you agreed to provide*).

You committed to ________________________________ (*outline the action steps the teacher will take*).

I will ________________________________ (*describe the follow up and accountability measures you will take including the date for each*)

I sincerely hope that as a result of these agreements, we will ________________________________ (*describe the desired state in terms of target teacher behavior and student achievement results*).

If you have any questions or concerns, my door is always open.

Sincerely,
Instructional Leader

**Meet with the teacher to share this letter and ask the teacher to sign it. Give one copy to the teacher and maintain one for your records.*

Sample Memorandum of Understanding

TO: Mr. Huckleberry
FROM: Mr. Boysenberry
DATE: March 19
RE: Follow up from our conversation dated March 18

DEAR MR. HUCKLEBERRY:

Thank you for taking the time to meet with me today to discuss the necessity that you conduct lab assignments in your chemistry class. The following is a summary of our conversation:

- It is important that you lead your students in conducting labs as an integral part of the chemistry curriculum.
- As of March 18, your students have not participated in any labs in your chemistry class. The district and state curriculum indicate that by now, your students should have conducted 8 such labs.
- You will need to make up the 8 labs that you have missed and conduct the remainder of the labs as outlined in the district and state curricular requirements.

In the course of our conversation, I committed to relieving you from your hall monitoring duties in order to allow you time to plan and prepare for the chemistry labs.

You committed to review the district and state curriculum, plan, prepare for, and conduct the 8 labs students missed by April 30, work with students after school to catch up on the curriculum, create a plan for how you will accomplish the other 4 labs by the end of the school year, and conduct all 12 of the required labs by the end of the school year. You will also work with the science coach to adjust your pacing so that you will have time to both cover the material and conduct the labs. Additionally, you committed to enrolling in curriculum training this summer at which you will adjust your course syllabus to accommodate the 12 labs for next year.

I will conduct an informal observation of your class each week and meet with you afterwards to discuss my observation notes as well as to review your lesson plans for the following week to provide you with feedback and to make sure that you remain on course.

I sincerely hope that as a result of these agreements, your chemistry students will all pass the district final exam and be prepared to enroll in AP chemistry the following year.

If you have any questions or concerns, my door is always open.

Sincerely,
Bob Boysenberry
Science Department Chair

Summary of the Four Strategic Conversations

	REFLECTING	FACILITATING
FEEDBACK	Feedback is reflective. You are simply summarizing what the teacher is saying.	Feedback is informative and solicited.
PROBLEM IDENTIFICATION	Teacher identifies challenge	Teacher identifies challenge
SOLUTIONS	Solutions are identified by the teacher	Solutions are identified by the teacher with some input from the leader
EVALUATION	The teacher sets the evaluation criteria and evaluates their progress through reflection.	The teacher evaluates his/her own progress and shares this information with the leader
IDEAL STATE	The teacher determines the ideal state	The teacher determines the ideal state with input from the leader
ROOT CAUSE	The teacher discovers the root cause through reflection	The leader asks the teacher probing questions in order to help the teacher see the root cause
SUPPORTS	The teacher identifies the supports he/she needs.	The teacher asks for support and the leader helps identify the types of supports that might meet the teacher's needs.
RESPONSES	Make *observations* that help the teacher look at his or her performance objectively.	Make *suggestions* that imply that present performance is okay and that the action is optional.

COACHING	DIRECTING
Feedback is focused on helping the teacher improve performance. Should be specific and timely.	Feedback provides information on how well the teacher is achieving the goals that were set. Feedback is based on agreed upon criteria.
Teacher and leader collaborative identify challenge	Leader identifies challenge
Solutions are collaboratively developed by the teacher and the leader	Solutions are identified by the leader.
The leader and the teacher evaluate the teacher's progress collaboratively	The leader evaluates the teacher's progress based on agreed upon criteria
The teacher and leader determine the ideal state together	The leader determines the ideal state.
The leader helps the teacher identify the root cause	The leader identifies the root cause and asks for feedback.
The leader and the teacher identify areas where the teacher may need support. The leader then suggests supports and the teacher chooses.	The leader asks the teacher what supports he or she might find useful in order to achieve the goal. The leader commits to provide these supports. The teacher commits to using them.
Make *recommendations* that signal that the teacher must change his or her current behavior but how that change is made is up for discussion. Be sure to follow up to ensure that the change is made.	Communicate *expectations* that signal that the teacher must change his or her current behavior. Stipulate how it must be done and in what time period.

Step Four

PUTTING IT ALL TOGETHER

Now that you have learned the four strategic conversations, it is time to put them together to create an overall approach for each teacher. Remember, it is not any one conversation that will make a difference; rather, it is the combination of conversational approaches that will help teacher make lasting improvements in their instruction. Thus, it is important to first figure out what kind of teacher you are facing and then map out a strategic conversational approach that will best meet the teacher's needs.

Mapping out your approach:

Because instructional leadership often takes a back seat to other responsibilities, it will be important to develop an instructional leadership plan and to track your progress throughout your plan. You will need to spend some time diagnosing your staff and then you will need to map out the best approach for each staff member.

Typically, your approach with each type of teacher will follow a predictable path.

LOW WILL/LOW SKILL

(Directive) → Reflective → Facilitative → Reflective → Coaching → Facilitative

LOW WILL/HIGH SKILL

Facilitative → (Directive) → Reflective → Coaching

HIGH WILL/LOW SKILL

Reflective → Coaching → Facilitative

HIGH WILL/HIGH SKILL

Reflective → Facilitative

Notice that the lower the will, the more you will have to work towards a relationship where you can be collaborative. At first, you will have to be more directive and to some degree, more hands off, focusing on specific teaching behaviors. As you develop trust and rapport you can move towards a coaching relationship that will address the underlying causes of those teaching behaviors and then work towards developing a skill set to address these behaviors. As teachers become more accustomed to growing in their skill and will, you can help them work to more autonomy through facilitation. Finally, as they become more adept, they will learn to reflect on their own and act on the information that the reflection reveals.

Although these paths are deceptively linear, they are not as straight forward as they appear. There will be times when you can skip a part of the process because the teacher with whom you are working becomes ready for more autonomy faster than you anticipated. Other times, you may need to revisit a prior conversational approach as you help teachers develop a new skill.

The key is to remain flexible. As you develop more proficiency with the strategic approaches, you will find that you will automatically shift to the right approach based on the nature of the conversation and the needs of the teacher with whom you are working. The more you practice strategic conversations, the easier it will be to quickly assess the situation and choose the right approach.

Where Do You Start?

In an ideal world, you would be able to begin work immediately with all of your teachers at once. But, in reality, you may not have the time or the resources to develop a strategic conversational approach with every teacher right away. You may have to decide with which teachers you will begin your work first and then add on others once you have developed your own proficiency and skill with strategic conversations. Platt, Tripp, Ogden, & Fraser (2000) suggest three criteria for selecting with which teachers you should begin. First, consider the degree of loss of student learning. Start with the teachers whose instructional practices have the most significant negative effect on student learning.

Next, consider your likelihood of success. Because the time you have to provide instructional leadership is limited, start with the teachers with whom you are most likely to make an impact most quickly. Once these teachers are on their way, you will free up time to deal with your most difficult cases.

Finally, consider the impact your instructional interventions will have on your institutional priorities. If for instance, your school's priority is increasing math scores on state-mandated high-stakes tests, you will need to start with those teachers who most impact the success or failure of this goal. In some cases, you may find that several teachers are facing the same instructional challenge and can be addressed as a group rather than as individuals.

You can use the worksheet on the following page to help you decide where to start.

Instructional Leadership Priorities Worksheet

List you top three school priorities for the year in order of importance:

1.

2.

3.

Rate the teachers you lead in each category on a scale of one to four.

TEACHER	**NEGATIVE IMPACT** (1= little or no impact. 4= great impact)	**LIKELIHOOD OF SUCCESS** (1= little or no likelihood. 4= great likelihood)	**IMPACT ON INSTITUTIONAL PRIORITIES** (1= little or no impact. 4= great impact)	**TOTAL**

Add up each teacher's score. Begin with the teachers with the highest score.

Tracking your progress

Once you have decided with which teachers you will work, it is important to track each teacher's growth. Doing so will not only help you decide what approach you should take next, it will help you assess the effectiveness of your choices so far. Use the template on the following page to help you track your progress.

Progress Tracking Sheet

Teacher Name: ______________________________

DATE	CONVERSATION	RESULT	FOLLOW-UP

Sample Completed Progress Tracking Sheet

Teacher Name: Mrs. Henderson

DATE	CONVERSATION	RESULT	FOLLOW-UP
9/15	Reflective: Pre-Observation Conf.	Learned objectives for course. Got a sense of will/skill	Observation and gather other data
9/30	Observation/ Reflective/ Facilitative	Made a commitment to work on pacing. Will follow up with informal obs. tied to pacing	Schedule 2 unannounced informal obs.
10/20	Reflective/ Coaching	Some dip in skill as Mrs. H attempted to apply pacing suggestions. Reflected on cause of difficulty and directed to other resources and will follow up.	Give Pacing suggestions from Skillful Teacher and follow up with brief reflection. 2 more unannounced informal obs.
12/5	Reflective/ Coaching	Acknowledged that pacing did help students stay on task.	Facilitative conversation to work on other classroom management issues.

Think About:

1. *Of the four teachers from the introduction, with which teacher would you start first? Why?*
2. *With which conversation would you start with Mrs. Henderson? Why?*
3. *What would your conversational plan look like for Mr. Locke? Why?*
4. *What will you have to do before Ms. Paulson is ready for a more collaborative approach?*
5. *Which conversational approach or approaches might you be able to skip with Mr. Terrell?*
6. *With how many teachers do you feel comfortable starting?*
7. *What will you need to do before you are ready to begin applying these approaches?*

Conclusion

MRS. HENDERSON

Mitchell walked out of Mrs. Henderson's fifth-grade classroom and headed back to his office. He had just completed a formal observation of her class and Mitchell was worried by what he saw. Mrs. Henderson spent the first 20 minutes of class taking attendance and collecting homework. Once she began her instruction, the students talked through the warm up, which had little to do with the posted objective. Most of the students were off task during the lesson activity and instead of helping them get back on task, Mrs. Henderson plowed through the lesson occasionally warning students that she would give them lunch detention if they didn't get their act together.

Mitchell knew that he would have to carefully plan the post-observation conference in order to make any progress. Mrs. Henderson was a veteran teacher who believed that she was effective in the classroom. Over the 18 years she had been teaching, she had received positive evaluations from her former principals. She often blamed the students for any difficulty she experienced. She was active in the teacher's union and had recently earned her EdD from a local university. After reviewing his notes, Mitchell decided he would begin the post-observation conference with reflective questions designed to help Mrs. Henderson think about her practice. He suspected that many of the classroom management problems stemmed from Mrs. Henderson's pacing so he decided he would transition to a facilitative conversation where he would share his observation notes paying particular attention to the timing and pacing of the lesson. Because she was a low will teacher who thought she was high will, he would have to help Mrs. Henderson make the connection between her teaching behavior and student success so she could commit to improving. Since Mrs. Henderson was resistant to help, he would facilitate rather than coach her in developing a solution to her pacing. Once they had a plan, he would promise to conduct a follow-up informal observation in two weeks. Mitchell knew that Mrs. Henderson would not like such feedback and would probably blame the students. But he was confident that by sharing the data and making her a partner in developing the solution, he would be able to get her focused on improving.

MR. LOCKE

Cassandra sat in her office stunned by what she had just heard. A parent had just called and reported that Mr. Locke, the AP chemistry teacher had not conducted one lab the entire year and it was February. The students would be facing the AP exam in just 3 short months and without doing any labs, they were desperately behind. Mr. Locke was a fairly new teacher and this was his first year teaching AP chemistry. He was enthusiastic and well-liked by the students and his colleagues. He worked hard at learning the curriculum and enthusiastically attended the professional development opportunities provided by the district. Earlier that year, he had struggled with classroom management but had worked hard to get his students focused on learning. Cassandra looked at the stack of papers waiting to be graded on her desk. She had her own classes to teach and her own students to manage. She didn't have time to teach Mr. Locke's classes too. She opened her email account and sent Mr. Locke an email requesting that he see her after school. She would first check with Mr. Locke to make sure that what the parent reported was true, and, if it was, she would need to have a directive conversation with Mr. Locke. She began carefully planning a directive conversation directing Mr. Locke to start conducting labs beginning next week. Because she didn't have the time or resources to provide the intensive coaching Mr. Locke needed, she would use a facilitative conversation where she could put Mr. Locke in touch with other resources. Cassandra shook her head as she reached for the phone to call the district curriculum coach and schedule time for her to come out later that week and work with Mr. Locke on catching up. They would have to act fast if they were going to help the students get ready for this test.

MS. PAULSON

Marla walked around the room and collected the left-over handouts. She had just finished presenting at the faculty meeting and she was livid. Weeks earlier, her principal had shared with her the dismal reading scores their students had earned on the last state test. She asked Marla, who was the reading specialist, if she would share a few reading strategies with the staff at the next faculty meeting. Marla had spent hours researching best practices, created handouts with strategies teachers could immediately use with their students, and put together a PowerPoint presentation with the school's data and a plan of action. The last part of the meeting was devoted to teachers working in small groups to develop a plan for how they would raise their students' reading scores this school year. All of the teachers were enthusiastic about the information and immediately got to work. All of the teachers except Ms. Paulson. Ms. Paulson read a magazine throughout most of the presentation and when the teachers began working in groups, Ms. Paulson reluctantly joined a group near where she was sitting but contributed little to the discussion. It had been that way all year. Ms. Paulson would do what was required but nothing more. Although Marla was infuriated, she knew she would have to get Ms. Paulson on board if their reading scores were going to improve. Marla decided to follow up with Ms. Paulson with a reflective conversation on the workshop. She would begin by seeking Ms. Paulson's feedback and then ask probing questions to uncover why Ms. Paulson was so resistant to the professional development. Based on what she discovered, she could choose either coaching or facilitating to help Ms. Paulson make improvements in her practice. "It's a least a start," Marla sighed as she packed her laptop. She headed to her office to plan her conversation.

MR. TERRELL

Scott scanned the latest test results and smiled. The scores were up overall but one teacher's scores really stood out. Mr. Terrell's students had outperformed the other students in their grade by 10 percentage points. "I'm not surprised," Scott chuckled. Mr. Terrell was one of those rare teachers you die to have in your building. Not only was he an excellent instructor, but he cheerfully took on any task he was assigned. He was a joy to have on the staff and made a tremendous difference in the lives of the students. Parents clamored to have their students in his class. Not only that, but Mr. Terrell sponsored the chess club after school and came in on the weekend to tutor students who needed extra help. Lately however, Mr. Terrell seemed a little bored. He still did whatever was asked of him but Scott sensed he needed a new challenge and worried Mr. Terrell would look for that challenge at another school. Scott decided to stop by Mr. Terrell's classroom after school to have a reflective conversation with him. He could help Mr. Terrell make connections between his practice and the students' success and perhaps unearth ways that Mr. Terrell might find more challenge and fulfillment in his current position. Based on that conversation, Scott could figure out how to facilitate other professional growth or even informal leadership opportunities for Mr. Terrell.

Strategic conversations will not operate in a tidy, linear fashion. As you are developing your skill at structuring and conducting strategic conversations you will make mistakes along the way. Things will not go as you planned or progress will take longer than you imagined. You will get frustrated from time to time, and some interactions will be so difficult and will yield such little immediate resolution that you will wonder why you even bothered putting in the time and effort to have the conversation in the first place. There will be some teachers who will resist your efforts. Others will play along at first in order to wait you out, hoping that you will give up at some point and just leave them alone.

It is during these times that you have to resolve not to give up. You have to stick with it. You have to return to the teacher with whom you just had the difficult interaction and try again. You have to analyze your mistakes and make plans to do better next time. You have to try another strategy and then another one when the first approach doesn't work. The power in strategic conversations is not in any one exchange with a teacher, although there will be times when one exchange will make a huge difference. The real power of strategic conversations is in the fact that they are ongoing. Little by little, you are helping teachers recognize the impact of their current instructional behavior on student achievement, and together you and the teacher are figuring out how to improve their instruction and thereby improve student achievement.

Remember, you cannot force change or commitment. People have to make the decision to commit. But, as Peter Senge (2000) points out,

> *...if you can't force commitment, what can you do? You can do the same things that a teacher does to foster genuine learning with students. You can nudge a little here, inspire a little there, provide a role model. Your primary influence is in the environment you create – an environment that encourages awareness and reflection, that gives people access to tools and training that they ask for, and that enables them to develop their own ability to make choices. (p. 273).*

Remaining engaged in strategic conversations over the long term allows you to you help others choose to make the commitment to their own professional growth.

That's because strategic conversations help you to build relationships, establish trust, break through resistance, alter tightly-held but erroneous beliefs about students and teaching, and plant the seeds of improvement. It doesn't happen after one interaction. That kind of dramatic change, the kind of dramatic change you are looking for, only happens bit by bit, over time. It isn't the result of one specific moment, but a series of moments, a succession of interactions. And, it only happens if you are tenacious. You have to stick with it even when it looks like nothing's happening.

As you begin to use strategic conversations, here are a few final tips to keep in mind.

- Make excellence the norm, not the exception. Base all your professional development efforts on the assumption that all teachers must (and can) perform at high levels. You cannot afford to allow teachers to slide by with mediocre or poor performance in your school. Every teacher must be expected to continually improve and move towards mastery teaching. If this becomes the norm in your school, if you base every interaction with teachers on this one assumption, then you can dramatically shift the culture of your school towards continuous professional improvement.
- Believe that all your teachers can improve even when the evidence speaks to the contrary. This belief is fundamental to your success working with teachers. In the same way that we believe all students can learn, we have to believe that all teachers can get better at teaching.

Even if you do not believe this now, work on altering your belief until you do. Decide that you will persist with every teacher with whom you work to help them improve their professional practice.

- The farther away a teacher is from being a reflective practitioner, the more hands-on you will have to be in order to scaffold their development towards reflection.
- Begin with the least intrusive strategy first. The only time you should default to a directive conversation is when the teacher's behavior is hurting students, or the teacher has already demonstrated that he or she is impervious to other approaches. Otherwise, choose a more interactive strategy, even if doing so will mean you have to move more slowly towards getting the results you want. Directive conversations will often foster compliance but rarely encourage buy-in from teachers. Therefore, you cannot afford to rely on directive conversations in any but the direst circumstances. Always begin with an approach that allows the teacher to take the ownership of developing a solution.
- If a teacher lacks either the skill or will to develop solutions, move to making recommendations but be careful to recommend steps that will have a direct impact on the teacher's behavior and ultimately on student achievement. Don't waste your time or the teacher's time by recommending actions that will not directly result in improving the teacher's condition or student achievement. Use the data to help you determine the core issue and then address the core issue first.
- As teachers make progress, be careful how you praise their efforts. Don't offer general praise (i.e. "great job!" or "you are making good progress") or commend their talent or abilities ("you're becoming a fabulous teacher" or "you're so talented"). Instead, point out specific teaching behaviors and praise teacher's efforts, processes, and choices that produced the behavior ("I noticed 10 more students were on task during my last visit! Putting the directions on the board seems to be really making a difference.") In that way, you are giving teachers powerful feedback they can use to continue their improvement.
- Offer feedback in ways that are non-judgmental. Rely on specific observable data as the basis for any feedback you share. Then engage teachers in a conversation about the impact their teaching choices have on student achievement. Finally, use the data as the basis for any suggestions, recommendations, or directives you provide. The plan or solution you develop during the conversation should be in direct response to the data.
- It should go without saying that any conversation you have with a teacher should be confidential. The fastest way to destroy trust is to break the confidentiality of the conversations without the teacher's knowledge or permission.
- Realize that many instructional challenges are part of a bigger institutional problem. Examine the ways that institutional practices may be supporting mediocre or poor teaching and work to change these as you work to help individual teachers improve.

Remember that having the strategic conversation is one of the most loving and supportive things you can do. Many people persist in behaviors that are unproductive because they are not aware of what they are doing or because they do not feel they have a viable alternative way of behaving. Strategic conversations help you make teachers aware of what they are doing, the impact that it is having on student achievement, and more effective alternative behaviors.

Often in pursuit of state-mandated or district outcomes, we forget that the teachers with whom we are working are an integral and human part of the process. But, strategic conversations remind us that our goals are never more important than the people through which we need to work in order to achieve them. As you are considering your strategic conversational approach, consider whether what you are about to do adds to or takes away from the dignity of the person in front of you. Always select an approach that honors the inherent dignity in all of the teachers you serve.

References

BARTH, R.S. (2005). "Turning book burners into lifelong learners." In R. Dufour, B. Eaker, & B. Dufour (Eds.) On common ground. The power of professional learning communities. (pp. 115-134). Bloomington, Indiana: National Education Service.

BLASE, J. & BLASE, J. (2004). Handbook of instructional leadership (2nd edition): How successful principals promote teaching and learning. Thousand Oaks, California: Corwin Press.

INTERACTION ASSOCIATES (2004). Facilitative leadership: Tapping the power of participation. Boston: Interaction Associates, Inc.

JACKSON, R. (2009). Never work harder than your students and other principles of great teaching. Alexandria, Virginia: ASCD.

PLATT, A.D., TRIPP, C.E., OGDEN, W.R. & FRASER, R.G. (2000). The skillful leader: Confronting mediocre teaching. Acton, Massachusetts: Ready Press.

SENGE, P. (2000). Schools that learn: A fifth discipline fieldbook for educators, parents, and everyone who cares about education. New York: Doubleday.

SINGLETON, G. & LINTON, C. (2006). Courageous conversations about race: A field guide for achieving equity in schools. Thousand Oaks, CA: Corwin Press.

THOMPSON, M. (2008). Leadership, balanced achievement, & accountability: Benchmarking to exemplary practice. Boone, North Carolina: Learning-Focused.

Appendix

WALKTHROUGH PROCESS
INFORMAL OBSERVATIONS
FORMAL OBSERVATIONS

The Walkthrough Process

A walkthrough is a structured process for gathering data. It provides a specific snapshot of classroom instruction. Walkthroughs are kept separate from teacher evaluations.

PURPOSE:

The purpose of the administrative walkthrough is to:

- Improve communication about teaching and learning
- Gather baseline information for the planning process
- Monitor progress towards implementation of an action plan
- Focus on and celebrate successes in a specific area
- Highlight areas that will need further improvement
- Foster self-assessment by individuals or groups
- Make the instructional leader visible
- Allows instructional leaders to address issues with teachers early on before they escalate

TYPES:

Leadership Walkthroughs: Short classroom visits conducted by a single administrator or instructional leader designed to gather a quick snapshot of individual classroom practice and offer specific, non-evaluative feedback as well as to develop a broader picture of classroom practice over time.

Collegial Walkthroughs: Short classroom visits conducted by a team of teachers to gather a data around a focus question [3].

Stakeholder Walkthroughs: Short classroom visits conducted by a team of stakeholders (i.e. school administration, staff, central office or district personnel, parents, partner organizations, and students) to gather information related to specific school progress goals.

3. For a complete guide for conducting walk-throughs as well as instructions, tools and templates for conducting collegial and stakeholder walkthroughs, visit www.mindstepsinc.com/resources.asp to order or download your copy of *The Walkthrough Toolkit: A Complete Guide for Conducting Walkthroughs.*

PROCESS FOR LEADERSHIP WALKTHROUGHS:

Before the Walkthrough:

The key to making walkthroughs work is to first make teachers comfortable with the idea that someone will be visiting their classrooms. Teachers will be skeptical at first. Ease their discomfort by making the process as transparent as possible.

1. Announce ahead of time that you will be visiting classrooms. Share with teachers that your visits will not be tied with the formal observation process.
2. Develop an area of focus ahead of time. Will you look for classroom management techniques, levels of rigor, questioning strategies, evidence of effective planning, etc.? Because your visit will be brief, select one or two discrete teaching skills tied to your school's target or goals for the year and only observe for these during your visit.
3. Decide what group you will focus on. Will you look at a particular department, grade level, team of teachers, or will you look for trends across the school?
4. Decide how you will collect data, use the data you collect, and how you will communicate it to the faculty.
5. Share your focus with teachers and the data collection tool you will be using. Explain how you will use the data you collect. Answer any questions they may have.
6. Decide which teachers you will be visiting. At the beginning, you may want to warn teachers ahead of time. After teachers are used to seeing you in the classroom, you can just stop by unannounced.
7. Make sure that you have copies of your data collection tool for each classroom you visit.
8. Decide how you will follow up with teachers after your walkthrough. Share this information with teachers as well.

During the Walkthrough:

1. Classroom visits should last 5-7 minutes each.
2. During the visit, record on the capture sheet any data you notice that relates to the focus question. Pay attention to: 1) room environment (how is the room organized for learning?), 2) student behavior (how do students demonstrate that they are learning?), 3) teacher behavior (how do teachers facilitate student learning and respond to students when they demonstrate that they are not learning?).
3. If it will not cause a disruption, talk to some of the students. Ask them what they are doing and why. Look to see that students understand what is being asked of them and how the activity relates to the posted objective of the class.
4. Look for other evidence of student learning such as student work and posted student grades.
5. Record your observations on the capture sheet.

After the Walkthrough:

1. Review your notes and look for trends and patterns both for the individual teacher and for the department, grade level, team, or school-wide. What implications does the data have for your own leadership and for the progress the teachers are making towards individual and school goals?
2. Determine how you will act on the data you have collected. Will you only follow up with teachers individually or will you share the general trends you have noticed with a larger group of teachers, your supervisor, or other specialists in the building?
3. Make sure that each teacher receives some feedback from your visit. Most walkthrough feedback should be brief and non-evaluative. Its purpose is to share data and set the stage for one of the strategic conversations. It could be in the form of a brief email or note or you can follow up verbally in a quick casual conversation later that day but do follow up shortly after your visit.
4. If a teacher requires more follow-up, schedule a time within 3 days to follow up with the teacher and develop a strategic conversation plan.
5. Schedule your next walkthrough.

More Guidelines

- Walkthroughs should be frequent in order for them to be effective. Plan to visit at least three classrooms per walkthrough and conduct at least one walkthrough per week (2-3 if you are an administrator).
- Walkthroughs are designed to be short. Do not stay in the classroom longer than 7 minutes. Otherwise you have moved into an informal observation.
- Walkthroughs work best when they have a specific focus. Although you can use walkthroughs more generally and simply visit classrooms to gather overall impressions, they are most helpful when there is a specific teaching behavior or set of behaviors you are observing.
- The best evidence of effective teaching is student learning. Therefore, all walkthrough participants should look for evidence of student learning in each classroom.

Walk-Through Capture Sheet

TEACHER NAME: ____________________

CLASS: ____________ PERIOD: ________ DATE: ________

ACQUISITION	APPLICATION
Students acquire knowledge and are primarily expected to remember or understand this knowledge.	Students use what they have learned to solve problems, develop solutions, and further refine thinking skills. The highest level of application is to apply knowledge to new and unpredictable situations.

RIGOR

ASSIMILATION	ADAPTATION
Students synthesize several thinking skills into thinking processes and are able to use these processes automatically and routinely to analyze and solve problems and create solutions within a particular subject.	Students take what they have learned and adapt it to fit new, unpredictable, or unrelated situations. They use their knowledge to create solutions to unfamiliar challenges and apply across disciplines.

Adapted from the Rigor and Relevance Framework by the International Center for Leadership in Education

Informal Observations

Although you are free to go into a classroom without an observation tool and provide informal comments after visiting a classroom, agreeing with teachers ahead of time on an observation tool makes it easier for you to provide targeted feedback and makes the process transparent and therefore less threatening to teachers. Using these tools also helps calibrate the feedback that teachers and you receive from the other instructional leaders in the building.

THE FOLLOWING TWO TOOLS WILL HELP YOU CONDUCT INFORMAL OBSERVATIONS.

The first tool is a checklist you can use when visiting classrooms. Make sure to vet this checklist with teachers ahead of time. Explain to them that the checklist helps them understand what teaching behaviors you are hoping to see. Tell them that just because something is not checked does not mean that they are not doing it in the classroom. With such a brief visit, not everything can be observed. Cast the checklist as a tool to help you capture what is working in the classroom rather than as a "gotcha" mechanism designed to record what is not happening. Make sure that you do this before you use the tool in the classroom and, shortly after you begin using the checklist, check in with teachers to see if it is providing them useful feedback and how it can be adjusted.

The second tool leaves things more open ended. Still, it is important that you vet it with teachers prior to using it. Solicit their suggestions for how the tool can be made more useful for them since the primary goal of informal observations is to provide teachers with feedback they can use to improve their performance.

The key to informal observations is that the feedback is immediate. Once you complete the form, leave it in the teacher's classroom when you leave. This will reduce the suspense teachers may feel after the observation and will provide them with instant feedback. If you feel you must keep the form, make a copy of the form and put it in teachers' boxes by the end of the day. These forms can also be printed on triplicate paper. In that case, you can retain one copy for your records and give the teacher two copies – one for their records and one on which they can provide a written response.

You can copy these tools right from this book. You can also download adaptable templates from our website at http://www.mindstepsinc.com/publications_sc.asp and fill them in with the standards from your particular school or district.

Informal Observation Form (Version A)

TEACHER NAME: ____________ OBSERVER NAME: ____________

DATE: ________ TIME: ________ PERIOD: ________

SUBJECT: ____________________

STANDARD 1: Demonstrated commitment to students and their learning.

- ☐ You review the previous lesson's homework
- ☐ You check for understanding
- ☐ You provide opportunities for critical and reflective thinking
- ☐ You demonstrate clear, positive expectations
- ☐ You take time to unscramble confusion
- ☐ Other: ____________________

STANDARD 2: Content and Pedagogical Knowledge

- ☐ You post instructional objectives stated in terms of student behaviors
- ☐ You use a variety of instructional strategies
- ☐ You provide lesson closure
- ☐ You provide opportunities for student practice
- ☐ You make connections to prior learning or other content
- ☐ The lesson activities match the mastery objective
- ☐ Other: ____________________

STANDARD 3: Classroom Management

- ☐ You greet students as they arrive to class
- ☐ You use a warm up activity
- ☐ You start instruction immediately
- ☐ You post the class agenda/ activities
- ☐ Materials and equipment are ready
- ☐ You use positive reinforcement
- ☐ You use appropriate behavior management strategies
- ☐ Student involvement is apparent
- ☐ Students are on task
- ☐ The classroom environment is reflective of the instruction that occurs
- ☐ The lesson maintains momentum and an appropriate pace
- ☐ Other: ____________________

STANDARD 4: Assessment

- ☐ You use a variety of formative assessment strategies to check for understanding
- ☐ You provide rubrics
- ☐ You clearly state the criteria for success
- ☐ You modify instruction is based on student feedback
- ☐ You match the method of assessment to the content
- ☐ Other: ____________________

COMMENTS:

Informal Observation Form (Version B)

TEACHER NAME: ______________________ **OBSERVER NAME:** ______________________

DATE: __________ **TIME IN:** __________ **TIME OUT:** __________ **CLASS:** __________ **PERIOD:** __________

EXPECTATIONS: How does the teacher communicate high expectations for all students? (will)	
INSTRUCTIONAL STRATEGIES: How does the teacher use instructional strategies to help all students master the content? (skill)	
CLASSROOM MANAGEMENT: How does the teacher organize the classroom environment to facilitate student learning? (skill)	
ASSESSMENT: How does the teacher assess student progress, analyze the results, and adapt instruction to improve student achievement? (skill and will)	

ADDITIONAL COMMENTS:

Not all standards may be observed during the brief informal observation visit.
Distribution: Top – Teacher, Middle – Administrator, Bottom - Observer

Formal Observations

The formal observation process is most likely dictated by your particular school district. What follows are a few tips to make that process easier for both you and the teacher.

BEFORE THE OBSERVATION:

- Schedule your visit with the teacher giving the teacher plenty of time to prepare for the observation. Because the formal observation is akin to a summative assessment, you want teachers to have the opportunity to do their best.
- Meet with the teacher briefly in a pre-observation conference to make sure that the teacher is clear on the observation process you will use. Answer any questions the teacher has and ask the teacher if there is something in particular the teacher would like for you to observe while you are there. In this way, you can make the process more transparent and collaborative.
- Ask the teacher to see the lesson plan ahead of time so that you have an idea of the teacher's intent for the lesson. During your observation, you will look for how well the actual lesson matches the lesson the teacher planned.
- Review the informal observation and walkthrough notes you have collected throughout the year. These notes will give you a sense of the teacher's progress and will help you select areas of focus for your formal observation.
- Gather all of your data collection tools and organize them. Be prepared to start taking notes within 1 minute of sitting down in the classroom.

DURING THE OBSERVATION:

- Arrive in the classroom a few minutes before the bell or transition to the lesson you will be observing. Note how the teacher interacts with students during the unstructured time or how the teacher manages the transition between one phase of the class and the next.
- Take literal notes (see the note-taking template on page 96). Try to write down everything the teacher and students say and do during your visit so that you can capture as much objective information as possible. Do not try to analyze teachers while they are teaching; you are likely to miss something. Later, you can analyze your notes and look for patterns. Literal notes will also allow you to share data with the teacher that will support your analysis of the teacher's performance.

- Select 3-5 random students and write down what they say and do in the class. Look for evidence that these students are learning.
- Pay attention to what is on the board, the walls, and other classroom displays. Describe or transcribe some of these in your notes and use these as further evidence of how teachers communicate their expectations to students. If the teacher is using a shared classroom space, note how the teacher adjusts the space for their particular class.
- In addition to the criteria on whatever form you are required to use, pay close attention to the following:
    - Who is doing the bulk of the work – the teacher or the students?
    - What work is the teacher doing and what work are the students doing?
    - Which students seem to be learning and how can you tell?
    - What evidence can the teacher give that the 3-5 random students you selected during your observation actually learned what they were supposed to learn during the period? What will the teacher do if they demonstrate that they did not learn what they were supposed to learn?
    - How does the teacher check to see that students are learning?
    - Can the level of student engagement be predicted by the students' race, gender, socioeconomic status, achievement level, seat in the classroom, or some other factor?

THE POST OBSERVATION CONFERENCE:

Use the post-observation conference as a way to collect more data rather than a time to pronounce your evaluation of the teacher's performance. Conduct the conference no more than 2 days after the observation. Before the conference, review your literal notes and look for patterns and evidence of the teacher's mastery of the teaching standards recommended by your school district but keep in mind that the real test of a teacher's skill is whether students learned what they were supposed to learn. Therefore, pay particular attention to those teaching behaviors that facilitated and /or inhibited student learning.

During the conference, share the data you have collected during the observation, ask questions, and allow teachers to interpret the data and draw conclusions. Spend most of your Take notes during the conference and include teacher responses to your feedback in your final write up.

The post observation conference is an excellent time to apply one or more of the strategic conversational approaches. However, because the post observation conference is a high stakes you may meet with some resistance or defensiveness on the part of the teacher. In order to keep the conversation on track, use the following strategies adapted in part from Senge (2000), p. 218.

WHEN...	YOU MIGHT SAY...
A teacher expresses strong views without providing their reasoning...	"I hear what you are saying but I'd like to understand more. What leads you to believe ...?"
The teacher tries to take the conversation off on a tangent...	"I am unclear how that connects to what we've been discussing. Can you show me how that is relevant?"
The teacher puts several things on the table at once...	"Okay, so far we have three things on the table (list them). Let's address them one at a time..."
The teacher takes a position but doesn't identify the concerns that led to his/her position...	"I understand that is your position. I would like to understand the concerns you have. Can you tell me what your concerns are?" and then..."How do you see that (your position) as the best way to resolve your concerns?"
The teacher's makes a point but it is unclear to you...	"What I understand you to be saying is... (restate what you think the teacher is saying). Is that accurate?"
The teacher uses a veiled or loaded phrase and you are not clear what he/she means by it...	"When you said (repeat the phrase), I typically use it to mean (share your interpretation). How are you meaning it?
The teacher makes an assertion about students but does not support it with data...	"What leads you to say that?" or "What data helped you come to that conclusion?"
A teacher seems entrenched in position.	"What would have to happen before you would be willing consider an alternative approach?"
You and the teacher reach an impasse	"It feels like we are getting into an impasses and I am afraid that we will walk away from this meeting without coming up with a viable solution. What can we do to move the conversation forward?"

Classroom Observation Note-Taking Sheet

TEACHER NAME: ______________ OBSERVER NAME: ______________

DATE: __________ TIME IN: __________ TIME OUT: __________

CLASS: ______________________________

TIME	TEACHER	STUDENTS	COMMENTS

Classroom Observation Note-taking Sheet Instructions

For a 30 minute classroom observation you will probably use between 8 and ten note-taking sheets.

Time column:

Make a note of the time next to every change in classroom activity or shift in teacher activity. At a minimum jot down the time every ten minutes or so next to whatever activity you are recording so that you can get a sense of the pacing of the class.

Teacher Column:

Write everything the teacher says verbatim in the teacher column (develop a shorthand to capture everything). If you miss something, use ellipses to indicate that there is missing information. Describe what the teacher is doing in parentheses next to the teacher's words when appropriate.

Student Column:

Record what the students say or do in the student column so that you can get a sense of how students respond to the teacher and vice versa. If you know the students' names, indicate which students said or did what. If you do not know the students' names, use a short-hand to describe the students in your notes. You can also draw a rough diagram of the classroom in the student column or on the back of the sheet before you begin. Then, you can reference students by location as you are taking notes. Count how many students are in the classroom and how many are on task and note that in the student column from time to time. Also note such things as how many students raise their hands to respond to teachers' questions, how many students follow directions the first time, or specific students' location in the classroom.

Comments Column:

During your observation, record any questions that you have about what is happening in the classroom in the comments column. You will raise these questions during the post-observation conference. After the observation, review your notes and make any comments, note any patterns, and write your analysis of what took place in the classroom in the comments column. You will use these to create your final observation report.

About Mindsteps Inc.

Mindsteps™ Inc. is an educational consulting firm that helps teachers, administrators, and school systems figure out how to help any teacher reach every student. We help our clients get to the root of what's not working and develop more effective ways to help ALL their students achieve.

Mindsteps™ Inc. has helped hundreds of teachers and administrators improve student achievement through its workshops, seminars, free materials, books, and consulting services. We use a simple set of timeless principles to help educators diagnose their challenges and develop an action plan to resolve them. We won't suggest a solution until we are clear about who you are and what it is you are facing. If you'd like our help, give us a call at 1-888-565-8881 or email us at info@mindstepsinc.com. The first consultation is free.

About Mindsteps Series

The Mindsteps Series™ is a workbook series designed to give teachers, instructional leaders, and administrators practical, step-by-step guidance to develop those skills most essential to good teaching. For more information or to view other titles in the series, visit our website at http://www.mindstepsinc.com. If you would like a Mindsteps Coach to work with your school or district on one of the Mindsteps Series™, please give us a call at 1-888-565-8881.

Want More?

If you'd like more information about how Mindsteps Inc. can help you or your team, visit www.mindstepsinc.com/Conversations. There you will find information on:

- Free teaching and leadership resources
- Tips and Strategies
- Free Monthly e-newsletter
- Book order information
- Video snippets of Robyn
- Podcasts

And much more reader-only content!

Mindsteps Inc. has helped hundreds of teachers and administrators improve student achievement through our workshops, seminars, free materials, books, and consulting services. We want to hear from you - share your success stories with us and read what others have to say at our website www.mindstepsinc.com.

About the Author

Robyn R. Jackson, PhD has been a teacher, administrator, researcher, consultant, and keynote speaker. As a National Board Certified English teacher, she increased the enrollment of minority and non-traditional students in her AP Language and Composition classes and tripled her overall course enrollment within one year without a decrease in her students' test scores. As a middle school administrator in Montgomery County Maryland, she has worked to revise the district's Gifted and Talented program to be more inclusive of all students and better prepare students for rigorous high school work. She also helped lead one of the largest middle schools in the district to state and national Blue Ribbon status. As an educator, she has served as an adjunct professor and presented her own research at several national conferences.

Because of her practical approach to instruction, Dr. Jackson has become a nationally recognized presenter and consultant who has been featured in The Washington Post, on several radio programs, a PBS/Annenberg television series, and Lifetime Television's Lifetime Live. She works regularly with schools throughout the United States, helping them build their capacity to meet the diverse needs of their students and to remove the institutional barriers to student success. In addition to working with non-profits such as The College Board, The National Governors Association, and The Fulfillment Fund, she has worked with school districts and state departments of education in the District of Columbia, Delaware, Maryland, Florida, Massachusetts, Wisconsin, Minnesota, Illinois, Georgia, Virginia, and Ohio on everything from improving the planning and delivery of instruction to developing the leadership capacity of the school leadership team. Recently, Dr. Jackson was named a fellow with the Phelps Stokes Fund to research ways to improve teacher preparation. She is the author of *The Differentiation Workbook, Never Work Harder than Your Students and Other Principles of Great Teaching*, and is currently working on her next book on seven essential leadership behaviors to promote equity, access, and rigor.

To learn more about her visit www.mindstepsinc.com. To invite her to speak at your next conference or professional development offering, contact her at robyn@mindstepsinc.com.